Low-Carb SLOW COOKING

Over 150 Recipes for the Electric Slow Cooker

Dominique DeVito

with Breea Johnson, M.S., R.D., L.D.N.

CIDER MILL PRESS

BOOK PUBLISHERS

Kennebunkport, Maine

13-Digit ISBN: 978-1604335064
10-Digit ISBN: 1604335068

This book may be ordered by mail from the publisher. Please include $3.95 for postage and handling.
Please support your local bookseller first!

Books published by Cider Mill Press Book Publishers are available at special discounts for bulk purchases in the United States by corporations, institutions, and other organizations. For more information, please contact the publisher.

Cider Mill Press Book Publishers
"Where good books are ready for press"
12 Spring Street
PO Box 454
Kennebunkport, Maine 04046

Visit us on the Web!
www.cidermillpress.com

Design by Alicia Freile, Tango Media
Typeset by Candice Fitzgibbons, Tango Media
Typography: Archer, Chaparral Pro, Helvetica Neue and Voluta
All images used under license from Shutterstock.com.
Printed in China

1 2 3 4 5 6 7 8 9 0
First Edition

Contents

Introduction

Going Low-Carb for Life—

With the Help of a Slow Cooker

*E*veryone wants to feel better, right? And everyone wants to look better, too. So who can resist the assurances of a diet that says you will be able to eat a wide range of foods, almost freely, and still improve your overall health while losing weight? It sounds too good to be true.

And it nearly is. Because truthfully, there are no magic formulas for improved health and weight loss (despite what some diet products and systems would have you believe). To reap the rewards of feeling and looking good, you need to understand what the sacrifices are—and commit to them.

A diet low in certain carbohydrates can and will help you feel and look better. The rewards of a low-carb diet include weight loss, increased energy, and controlling diabetes. There are definitely sacrifices, though. If the sight, smell, and taste of a freshly baked loaf of bread is one of life's greatest pleasures for you, or if you can't imagine a week without pasta, or if you've been eating a bowl of cereal for breakfast every day since you were in first grade, you will be tested. Every day. And here's some of the hardest news: If you want to continue to feel and look better, you can't revert to your carb-loaded days. If you do, the weight will come right back.

The best way to be successful on a low-carb diet is to start at home. Go through your pantry, your cabinets, your fridge, and your desk drawers and other food hiding places, and get rid of all the foods you should no longer be eating. Then stock up on foods that are allowed. This is covered in depth in Chapter 1.

Next, get creative with those ingredients. If you limit your menus to the same things over and over, you'll get bored fast. And it's really not good for you. When the Atkins Diet first hit the scene back in the 1980s, it didn't seem right that people could eat bacon and eggs for breakfast day after day, or that the fat content of the cheese didn't matter. And while these things were part of the diet—and people were losing weight like crazy—it wasn't a realistic way of eating. It sounds easy and satisfying to regularly eat foods that were cautioned to be eaten in moderation for years (things like eggs, bacon, processed cheese, red meat, and artificial sweetener), but after a while, it's not.

Remind yourself as you're starting out that it's not really things like bagels, baked potatoes, orange juice, or ice cream that are the enemies, it's boredom from eating the same low-carb foods over and over again that will get you. And that's where your slow cooker and this book will help. Many carb-laden foods are simple to eat and extremely satisfying. They make meals easier—pizza, pasta, even peas and carrots. If you don't want to be agonizing about what to make for dinner on the nights when your time and energy are limited, with the slow cooker you can practically pull things from the cabinet, put them in the pot, and let them slow cook while you're at work. When you get home, you'll have a delicious dinner made with the right ingredients.

About Carbs and How to Count Them

Carbohydrates are the nutritional component in certain foods that provide fuel for the body. There are several types of carbohydrates—starches, sugars, and fiber—and they are categorized as simple or complex. These are found naturally in foods as varied as grains, beans, vegetables, fruits, and even milk. The sugars and starches in carbohydrates break down during digestion and are absorbed as blood sugar (glucose) in the bloodstream. Glucose enters cells with the help of insulin, and the glucose is used by the body for energy. What's not used is stored in cells as well as in muscles and in the liver, and if it's not used up, it's converted to fat. Eating a low-carb diet will cause the body to burn the fat reserves rather than create more fat.

The results are demonstrated: Weight loss will occur on a low-carb diet. Blood sugar levels decrease. The objective is not to go to the extreme, though, and cut off carbs. Carbs are, in fact, an essential element to overall good health. Dropping them too quickly can have side effects like headache, fatigue, nausea, and constipation.

Another key to a successful low-carb diet is learning to understand your carb intake. You need carbs, and they are present in so many foods! It's whether the carbs are simple or complex that matter, because that's going to determine how quickly they end up as fat reserves in the body. Simple carbs are very easily digested and thus go more quickly to being stored as fat. The easiest way to determine the complexity of a carb is to think about how "whole" it is. Processed foods are the biggest offenders. Then there are foods like white bread, rice, crackers, sugar (baked goods), and so on. Disappointingly, even white potatoes fall into this category.

Complex carbs are those with minimal processing or whose fiber content is significant. Think leafy and cruciferous vegetables, lean sources of protein, fish, and whole seeds. In Chapter 1, we'll examine the ingredients you need to have on hand in your low-carb pantry, which will make meal planning much easier. The bottom line is that you want your body to be able to use the food it eats for energy in a way that generates the least amount of reserves stored as fat. Using a slow cooker to help with a diet like this turns simple ingredients into indulgent dishes. Good luck, and feel great!

Chapter 1

Stocking the Low-Carb Pantry

*C*ongratulations on your commitment to a low-carb diet. It's a big decision, and you'll need some help along the way—from these recipes and from your slow cooker. Think of it as a journey down a road you've never traveled. There's definitely a sense of adventure.

You may also have a sense of apprehension. You may be busy with work and family commitments and not used to making yourself—or what you eat— much of a priority. And so you need a road map to make the journey as easy as possible.

Going back to the travel analogy, you don't want to go down an unfamiliar road on a nearly empty tank of gas. What if you run out and you have no idea where you are? Being prepared is the first step. Before you get out any pots and pans or consider your first low-carb meal, you need to rid your house of as many high-carb foods as you can.

The Bad Guys

There are some foods that are easy to recognize as completely detrimental to low-carb eating. Consider these the potholes on your new journey. Very simply, they are white and processed: white bread, sugar, cookies, milk, chips, canned soups, potatoes, breakfast cereals, muffins, bagels, and pasta. Avoid foods with any of these ingredients:

✱ Sugar

✱ High-fructose corn syrup

✱ Starch

✱ Refined flour

✱ Trans fats (hydrogenated or partially hydrogenated oils)

Assessing Carb Content

You're probably familiar with obvious culprits like white bread, potato chips, processed baked goods, and white flour-based pastas, but were you surprised to find milk or canned soups on the list of bad guys? There will be a lot of foods you'll wonder about, so it's helpful to understand what you want to accomplish with your carb intake so you can make the best choices.

There are multiple theories about how many carbs to eat in a day. Carbs do, after all, fuel the body and brain, and without them, you can experience fatigue, nausea, and even disorientation. In fact, the brain is a carb guzzler; you need carbs! In 2010, the Dietary Guidelines for Americans recommended that carbohydrates make up 45 to 60 percent of one's daily caloric intake—about 300 grams a day on a 2,000-calorie diet. The Recommended Daily Allowance for carbs is 130 grams. And, in fact, this quantity is consistent with a low-carb diet. Low-carb diets recommend that you limit daily carb counts to between 50 and 100 grams—the fewer the better, especially in the early stages.

The carbohydrate content is one of the requirements on a nutrition label, but not all foods have labels, and they can be a bit tricky to read. That's because fiber is a component of carbohydrates, and the grams of fiber should be subtracted from the total carb count as they're considered beneficial. That's why books dedicated to the low-carb lifestyle contain information on determining the net carb content of a food and using that as the number to count when adding up your daily intake.

Fortunately for us, the low-carb diet has been studied long enough that there are things we can now take for granted so it's not necessary to count every carb. These things include the list of "bad guys" laid out earlier. Like the popular anti-drug phrase coined in the 1980s goes, "Just Say No" to foods that fall into the "bad guys" category. Get them out of your house to the best of your ability.

Lots of Good Guys

Let's focus now on the foods you can eat. These are the ones you'll want to keep in stock so that you can put together healthy snacks and meals quickly and know you're staying the low-carb course with your diet.

To help you stock up on these meal builders, I've separated them into those that should be in the refrigerator (because they're perishable) and those that belong in the pantry (non-perishable).

In the Refrigerator (Perishable)

Meats:
* Cuts of lean beef
* Ground beef (90% lean is best)
* Veal
* Chicken pieces
* Whole chicken
* Turkey pieces
* Ground turkey
* Pork roast
* Pork chops
* Bacon
* Sausage
* Lamb
* Lamb chops
* Fish: lean fish like cod, perch, sea bass, flounder, and catfish; and fatty fish like salmon, tuna, sardines, and trout
* Shellfish: shrimp, clams, lobster, crabs, mussels, and oysters
* Eggs

Fresh vegetables:
* Leafy greens, including all lettuces, spinach, kale, chard, dandelion leaves, bok choy, endive, radicchio, watercress, and arugula
* Broccoli
* Brussels sprouts
* Cauliflower
* Celery
* Eggplant
* Fennel
* Garlic
* Ginger
* Green beans
* Mushrooms
* Onions
* Peppers
* Radishes
* Squash
* Tomatoes
* Turnips
* Zucchini

Fruits:
* Apricot
* Avocado
* Cantaloupe
* Coconut (unsweetened, of course)
* Honeydew
* Lemons
* Limes
* Passionfruit
* Pineapple
* Watermelon

Dairy:
* Cheese
* Butter
* Cream
* Half-and-half
* Unsweetened soy, coconut, or almond milks
* Unsweetened yogurt

Other: Raw wheat germ (refrigerate to keep fresh)

In the Pantry (Non-Perishable)

* Chicken broth
* Beef broth
* Bottled chilis
* Chipotle peppers bottled in adobo sauce
* Anchovies or anchovy paste
* Canned tomatoes
* Spaghetti sauce (no sugar added)
* Vinegar
* Mayonnaise
* Worcestershire sauce
* Tamari (soy sauce alternative)
* Fish sauce
* Unsalted nuts and seeds (almonds, hazelnuts, sunflower seeds, pumpkin seeds)
* Unsweetened coconut flakes
* Flaxseed
* Unsalted nut butters, such as natural peanut butter, almond butter, sunflower butter, sesame butter
* Oils (olive, canola, sunflower, and safflower oils)
* Toasted sesame oil
* Coconut oil

* Olives
* Roasted red peppers
* Tabasco sauce or other sugar-free hot sauces
* Chili garlic paste

Herbs and Spices: anything without sugar (including artificial sweeteners) or excessive sodium, but especially fresh or dried:
* Basil
* Cayenne
* Cilantro
* Cloves
* Coriander
* Cumin
* Curry
* Herbes de Provence blend
* Oregano
* Parsley
* Pepper
* Sage
* Salt
* Tarragon
* Thyme
* Turmeric
* Vege-sal

Flour and baking substitutes:

* Brans (wheat, oat, and rice brans)
* Almond meal, hazelnut meal (homemade is best; ½ to ¾ cup nuts = 1 cup flour)
* Oat flour
* Protein powder, especially rice
* Rolled oats
* Guar or xanthan gums (thickeners)
* Low-carb baking mixes (use in limited quantities; good for breading meats)
* Tapioca

Beverages:

* Water
* Wine
* Fruit-2-O

Sugar and Nutrition in General

Sugar is in many of the foods we eat (even some of our favorite fruits), and it's addicting. According to the 2010 Dietary Guidelines for Americans, "Added sugars contribute an average of 16 percent of the total calories in American diets. Added sugars include high fructose corn syrup, white sugar, brown sugar, corn syrup, corn syrup solids, raw sugar, malt syrup, maple syrup, pancake syrup, fructose sweetener, liquid fructose, honey, molasses, anhydrous dextrose, and crystal dextrose." Not only are these sugars contributors of detrimental carbohydrates, consumed in the quantities typical of an American diet, they're just not good for you.

Because we Americans like things sweet, many sugar substitutes have been introduced, both natural and artificial. Artificial sweeteners have been shown to actually increase appetite. Like plain sugar and high-fructose corn syrup, these artificial sweeteners should be completely avoided: Splenda, Equal, and aspartame. Agave syrup is touted as a "natural" non-sugar sweetener. It's from the agave plant. But it, too, is full of carbs and should not be consumed on a low-carb diet.

Of the natural sugar alternatives—and these should be used sparingly—consider unsweetened applesauce (28 grams/cup); pure maple syrup (67 grams/tablespoon); and raw honey (82 grams/tablespoon). Our feeling is that it's best to eat something real like raw honey that has many nutrients even if its carb count is high than satisfying your sweet tooth with a synthetic sweetener, even if the carb count is very low. The idea is to wean yourself off sugars to the best of your ability.

Take heart that dark chocolate (with a cocoa content of 75% or higher) is a sweet that can be used in moderation on a low-carb diet.

With your fridge and pantry stocked with low-carb ingredients, it's time to get cooking! Remember the new road/new journey analogy. You're going to come up against obstacles that threaten to deter you and take you off course, or leave you reeling from hitting a pothole. But hang in there. If weight loss is your goal, you'll be happy with the results if you diligently make low-carb choices. If you're currently overweight, weight loss will mean less strain on your heart, less strain on your joints, improved energy, and overall improved health. You can do it—and your slow cooker can help.

Chapter 2

Breakfast to Fuel the Body

When you're new to a low-carb diet, trying to decide what to have for breakfast can be almost painful! Gone are the go-to, easy choices of toast, a bagel, cereal, or a cereal bar. Pastries, croissants, pancakes, coffee cake—all gone. It's enough to make you want to kick your resolve to the curb.

Well, fear not. There are actually some low-carb baked goods you can make to satisfy your cravings. But, more importantly, we'll welcome some new choices that are going to result in a new you. You'll discover you have more energy and you'll feel full longer. Breakfast will indeed be the best fuel for your body to get off to a good start. Here goes!

Slow-Cooked Eggs

This is as simple as it gets. Unlike hard-boiling your eggs on the stovetop, you don't have to worry about the water boiling over.

8 to 12 eggs (depending on how many fit in one layer on the bottom of your slow cooker)

Large bowl of ice water

1. Place the eggs gently on the bottom of the slow cooker, being sure they are in a single layer. Add tap water to cover. Cover and cook on High for 2 hours.

2. When cooked, remove with tongs and place into bowl of ice water. Let the eggs stay in the ice bath for a couple of minutes. This reduces the temperature and loosens the shell for easy peeling.

Hard-boiled eggs make great snacks. Sprinkle with black pepper, garlic powder, paprika, or even a splash of hot sauce. Enjoy!

Egg Bake with Spinach and Mushrooms

This dish will feed a crowd—or you for a couple of days, which isn't such a bad thing!

Serves 10 to 12.

2 tablespoons olive oil

1 onion, chopped fine

1 cup sliced domestic mushrooms

4 cups spinach leaves, coarse stems removed, and ripped or cut into smaller pieces

12 eggs

½ cup half-and-half

½ cup unsweetened soy milk

1 tablespoon chopped fresh parsley

Salt and pepper to taste

1. Lightly grease the inside of the slow cooker with a teaspoon of the olive oil. In large skillet, cook onion and mushrooms in remainder of olive oil until tender. Turn the heat off, place the spinach leaves over the mixture, and cover with a tight-fitting lid. Allow the spinach to steam under the lid for about 10 minutes, which will cause it to wilt.

2. In a large bowl, beat the eggs with the half-and-half and soy milk until well mixed. Add the onion, mushroom, and spinach mixture, then the parsley, and stir just to combine.

3. Pour the eggs and vegetables into the slow cooker, cover and turn on low. Cook for 1 to 2 hours, until eggs are thoroughly cooked. To test for doneness, insert a clean knife in the center. If it comes out clean, the dish is ready.

This is delicious served with a fresh salsa. Chop 2 very ripe tomatoes and put them in a small bowl. Add a squirt of lime juice, a tablespoon of finely minced onion, 1 clove of crushed garlic, and a teaspoon or so of chopped jalapeno pepper (or a spicy pepper of your choice). Season with pepper and just a dash of salt.

Broccoli Frittata

Colorful, flavorful, and filling, this is a great way to get lots of low-carb nutrition from eggs and broccoli and enjoy every mouthful.

Serves 6.

2 tablespoons olive oil

1 medium onion, chopped

2 cloves garlic, minced

½ red or green bell pepper, seeds and ribs removed, thinly sliced

8 large eggs

3 tablespoons water

2 tablespoons fresh chopped parsley

1 tablespoon fresh thyme

¾ cup fresh broccoli florets, cut into bite-sized pieces

1. Heat the olive oil in a skillet and add onion, garlic, and bell pepper. Cook over medium-high heat until onion is translucent, about 3 minutes.

2. In a large bowl, whisk eggs with water, then add herbs and broccoli pieces. Add the cooked vegetables. Take a large piece of parchment paper, fold it in half, and place it in the slow cooker so the sides come up the sides of the cooker. This will give you a way to lift out the egg dish when it is cooked. Pour the egg mixture in on top of the parchment paper.

3. Cover and cook on High for about 1 hour or on Low for closer to 2 hours until eggs are set.

4. Run a spatula along the sides of the cooker to loosen the parchment paper. Lift the frittata out of the cooker with the paper, and slide it onto a serving plate.

> **Broccoli is loaded with Vitamin C and dietary fiber.**

Garden Vegetable Eggs

Besides making a wonderful breakfast, this colorful egg dish can also be served as a light lunch or dinner with a big salad using some of the same vegetables!

Serves 6 to 8.

2 tablespoons olive oil

1 onion, chopped fine

1 small zucchini, chopped

1 small green pepper, deseeded and chopped

2 ripe plum tomatoes, chopped

¼ cup chopped fresh basil

8 eggs

½ cup water

Salt and pepper to taste

1. Lightly grease the inside of the slow cooker with a teaspoon of the olive oil. In large skillet, cook onion, zucchini, and pepper until just tender, about 5 minutes. Add the tomatoes and basil and stir to heat through. Remove from heat.

2. In a large bowl, beat the eggs and water until well mixed. Add the vegetable mixture, and stir just to combine. Pour the eggs and vegetables into the slow cooker, cover and turn on low. Cook for 1 to 2 hours, until eggs are thoroughly cooked. To test for doneness, insert a clean knife in the center. If it comes out clean, the dish is ready.

Eggs Benedict: Create a gourmet low-carb version of eggs Benedict by serving this yummy egg dish on top of a slice of low-carb toasted bread, with a piece of grilled Canadian bacon and a dollop of homemade hollandaise sauce. When the egg dish has about a half hour left, make the hollandaise by whisking 3 egg yolks with 1 tablespoon each water and lemon juice in a small saucepan until well combined. Put the saucepan over low heat and keep mixing, cooking for about 5 minutes until mixture gets frothy and light. Remove the pan from the heat and stir in 6 tablespoons of butter, one at a time. Season with salt and pepper and a dash of cayenne.

Corned Beef Hash

The cauliflower in this recipe is so much more nutritious than potatoes, and it has a lighter, fresher flavor. Splash some hot sauce on it for extra zing.

Makes 2 to 4 servings.

3 tablespoons butter

¼ cup onion, chopped fine

1 clove garlic, minced

2 cups cauliflower florets, diced

1 pound corned beef, shredded

¼ cup chicken broth

Salt and pepper to taste

Non-stick cooking spray

1. In a skillet over medium-high heat, melt the butter. Add the onion and garlic and cook, stirring, until the onion is wilted, about 1 minute. Stir in the cauliflower pieces and stir, warming them through. Remove the pan from the heat.

2. Coat the inside of the slow cooker with non-stick cooking spray, and put the cauliflower mixture inside. Stir in the corned beef. Pour the chicken broth over everything. Cover and cook on Low for 1 hour or on High for about 30 minutes. Season with salt and pepper to taste. Serve hot.

Variation:

* Corned Beef Hash and Eggs: For an even more filling breakfast, add eggs. Simply crack two eggs open over the hash mixture in the slow cooker before cooking. They will cook along with the hash. Factor in an additional 20 to 30 minutes on Low or 15 to 30 on High.

Early Riser Poached Salmon

There are many cultures that eat fish for breakfast. Smoked salmon with cream cheese and bagels is a popular brunch menu selection. But for low-carb folks, this poached salmon kicks the excess calories of the other combo to the curb. For good.

Makes 4 to 6 servings.

6 cups water

1 medium onion, chopped

2 stalks celery, chopped

4 sprigs parsley

½ cup freshly squeezed lemon juice

8 whole black peppercorns

1 bay leaf

5-lb fillet or 4 small steaks of salmon

1 small lemon, sliced, for garnish

2 tablespoons fresh parsley, chopped, for garnish

1. To prep the poaching liquid, combine water, onion, celery, parsley, lemon juice, peppercorns, and bay leaf over medium heat. Bring to a boil and simmer for 30 minutes. Strain and discard solids.

2. Take a large sheet of heavy duty aluminum foil and place it inside the slow cooker so the sides emerge over the top. Press it into place so it conforms with the inside of the cooker. Turn the cooker on to High and, uncovered, let it preheat. Place the salmon over the foil in the slow cooker. Pour the hot poaching liquid over the salmon. Cover immediately, and cook on High for 1 to 2 hours until the flesh of the salmon is cooked through to a light pink but firm color and consistency.

3. Remove stoneware from slow cooker. Allow salmon to cool for 20 minute before transferring to a platter and serving. Garnish with lemon slices and fresh parsley sprigs.

This is a really tasty and satisfying breakfast after a workout, especially an early morning run. Imagine coming home home to a fragrant, succulent piece of hot salmon. Mmm.

Green Eggs and Ham

Breakfast is an important meal, especially for children, who need the protein to stay alert and focused until lunchtime. Serve this with a side of your favorite Dr. Seuss to get the day off to a great start.

Makes 2 to 4 servings.

1 tablespoon olive oil

½ small onion, minced

¾ cup cooked low-sodium ham, cut into pieces

6 eggs

½ cup water

½ cup steamed spinach, chopped, excess water squeezed out

2 tablespoons fresh parsley, chopped

Salt and pepper to taste

1. In a small skillet, heat the olive oil over medium-high heat. Add the onions and sauté until tender and translucent, about 3 minutes. Add the ham to coat with the oil and brown slightly, about a minute. Remove from heat.

2. In a large bowl, beat the eggs with the water until well blended. Add the spinach and parsley, and whisk to combine everything well and break up the spinach pieces.

3. Place the ham and onion mixture in the slow cooker, and pour the eggs over top. Cover and cook on Low for about 1 hour, until the eggs are cooked through. Season with salt and pepper when serving.

The Dr. Seuss book *Green Eggs and Ham* was produced as a result of a bet between the prolific author/illustrator and his equally accomplished editor, Bennett Cerf. Cerf's challenge was that Seuss use no more than 50 words in the entire book.

Crustless Quiche

This delicious mushroom and onion concoction is rich with tangy earth flavors and sweet, caramelized onions.

Makes 4 to 6 servings.

4 tablespoons unsalted butter

½ cup Vidalia onion, sliced into ribbons

2 cups sliced fresh mushrooms (this can be any kind of mushrooms from domestic to Portobello, crimini, shiitake, or any combination)

½ teaspoon dried sage

Salt and pepper to taste

10 eggs, beaten

1 cup half-and-half

1 cup shredded reduced-fat Swiss cheese

1. In a skillet over medium-high heat, melt the butter. Add the onions and stir until wilted, about 2 minutes. Add the mushroom slices and stir, cooking, until they start to soften and shrink, about 5 minutes. Remove from heat. Drain any liquid produced by the mushrooms. Stir in the sage, and season with salt and pepper.

2. In a bowl, beat the eggs. Add the half-and-half and the cheese, and then add the mushroom and onion mix.

3. Transfer everything to the slow cooker. Cover and cook on Low for 4 hours, being careful not to overcook. Serve hot.

If you want to add meat to this recipe, sauté some turkey bacon until crumbly. Add it to the mushroom mixture before cooking, or sprinkle it on top at the end.

Chapter 3

Low-Carb Soups and Stews

*S*oups and stews are some of the dishes most commonly made in a slow cooker, for obvious reasons! Because the moisture from the meats and vegetables is retained in the slow cooker, there is always additional liquid created in the cooking process—and this is what soups and stews are all about, that delicious liquid. The recipes in this chapter are chock-full of low-carb goodness, rich with vegetables, meat, and fish. You won't miss the grains or potatoes, either. Soup is food you can always feel good about eating, and once you start making it regularly you'll find that there are many ways to vary the basic ingredients.

Note: Many of the recipes call for the addition of a carrot. These add great flavor and nutritive value to soups and stocks. Carrots are a higher-carb vegetable, however. The quantities are minimal in these recipes, but they are present. You can choose to make the recipe without the carrot(s), scoop the pieces out before serving, or, if you're in a later stage of the diet, choose to keep them in the recipe.

Chicken Stock

Besides being the base of so many recipes, homemade stock is in and of itself an amazing food. Made with all parts of the chicken (or beef, or fish), a slow-cooked stock is rich in many minerals essential to good health, including calcium, magnesium, phosphorous, silicon, sulphur, and even glucosamine and chondroitin, which we often pay a lot of money for as a supplement for joint care! It is prized around the world as a remedy for whatever ails you, from digestive upset to sore throats to low libido. (Note: The amounts in this recipe are for a larger slow cooker; if yours is small, cut the recipe in half.)

Makes about 12 cups.

1 whole free-range chicken,
or 2 to 3 pounds of the bony parts
(necks, backs, breastbones, legs, wings)

Gizzards from the chicken

2 to 4 chicken feet (optional but beneficial)

1 large onion, chopped

2 carrots, peeled and sliced

2 celery stalks, chopped

4 quarts cold water

2 tablespoons vinegar

1 bunch parsley, chopped

1. If you are using a whole chicken, cut off the neck, wings, and legs and cut them into pieces. Cut the rest of the chicken pieces into chunks.

2. Place chicken pieces in the slow cooker and top with all vegetables except the parsley. Cover with water and vinegar. Cover, and let the meat and vegetables sit in the liquid for 30 minutes to 1 hour.

3. Turn the slow cooker to High and cook for 2 to 3 hours, or until boiling. Remove the cover and spoon off and discard any "scum" that has risen to the top.

4. Replace the cover and reduce the heat to Low. Cook for 8 to 10 hours. Add the parsley in the last 15 minutes or so.

5. When cooking is complete, remove the solids with a slotted spoon into a colander over a bowl. Any drippings in the bowl can go back into the stock. Remove any meat from the bones and eat separately.

6. Transfer the stock to a large bowl and refrigerate. When the fat is congealed on top, remove it, and transfer the stock to several smaller containers with tight-fitting lids. Stock can be stored in the refrigerator for several days, or kept frozen.

For a browner, even richer stock, place the chicken pieces on a cookie sheet. Preheat the oven broiler, and broil for about 3 minutes per side, until browned.

Beef Stock

This stock will add new layers of delicious complexity to recipes—and will make your kitchen smell fantastic while it's cooking.

Makes about 10 cups.

2 lbs beef marrow bones

2 lbs meaty rib or neck bones

3 quarts water

¼ cup vinegar

1 large onion, chopped

2 large carrots, chopped

2 celery stalks, chopped

3 sprigs of fresh thyme

1 teaspoon peppercorns

1 bunch parsley

1. Place the beef bones in a large pot and cover with water and vinegar. Let stand for one hour.

2. Place the meaty bones in a roasting pan. Preheat the oven to 350 and roast until well browned, about 30 to 40 minutes.

3. Place the soaked beef bones and the browned pieces in the slow cooker. Add the vegetables, thyme, and peppercorns, and cover with the water.

4. Discard the fat from the roasting pan, and fill with an inch or so of water. Place the pan over a burner on medium-high heat, and as the water heats, stir to loosen the coagulated juices and browned bits. Add this to the slow cooker. The water should just cover the meat and vegetables; add more if it doesn't.

5. Turn the slow cooker on High and cook for 2 to 3 hours until liquid is boiling. Remove lid and scoop out and discard scum that has risen to the top.

6. Replace the lid, lower the heat to Low, and cook for 12 to 18 hours—the longer, the better. Add the parsley during the last 15 minutes.

7. When cooking is complete, remove the solids with a slotted spoon into a colander over a bowl. Any drippings in the bowl can go back into the stock. Remove any meat from the bones and eat separately.

8. Transfer the stock to a large bowl and refrigerate. When the fat is congealed on top, remove it, and transfer the stock to several smaller containers with tight-fitting lids. Stock can be stored in the refrigerator for several days, or kept frozen.

Before you begin, be aware that stocks cook slower—that is, all day.

Fish Stock

The carcasses of fish typically have the filets removed already. A good fishmonger should have plenty to sell you at a modest price. Be sure to get the heads , too, as they are rich in iodine and fat-soluble vitamins.

Makes about 10 cups.

2 tablespoons clarified butter

2 onions, chopped

1 carrot, chopped

½ cup dry vermouth

3 quarts cold water

¼ cup vinegar

3 sprigs fresh thyme

Several sprigs fresh parsley

1 bay leaf

2 or 3 whole carcasses from non-oily fish such as snapper, rockfish, sole, or cod

1. In a large skillet over medium heat, melt butter and add onions and carrots. Cook for a couple of minutes at the higher heat to coat the vegetables, then reduce the heat to low and cook, stirring occasionally, until vegetables are soft, about 30 minutes. Add the vermouth and increase the heat to bring to a near boil.

2. Place the carcasses in the slow cooker. Cover with the water and vinegar. Add the vegetable mixture and bay leaf.

3. Cover and cook on High for 4 to 5 hours until liquid is boiling. Remove the cover and scoop off and discard the scum that has risen to the top.

4. Replace the cover and cook on Low for 10 to 18 hours—the longer the better.

5. When cooking is complete, remove the solids with a slotted spoon. Transfer the stock to a large bowl and refrigerate. When the fat is congealed on top, remove it, and transfer the stock to several smaller containers with tight-fitting lids. Stock can be stored in the refrigerator for several days, or kept frozen.

Make a more delicate seafood stock using lobster bodies from which the claws and tail have been removed. For this recipe, use 3 to 4 lobster bodies, or the bodies of 2 lobsters and the shells from 2 to 4 pounds of raw shrimp.

Mushroom Madness

A variety of mushrooms cooked with thick, meaty bacon contributes to the rich flavor of this delightful soup, which is especially good on cold winter days.

Serves 6 to 8.

6 pieces thick-cut bacon, diced

½ cup chopped yellow onion

½ teaspoon dried sage

¼ teaspoon cayenne pepper

½ lb fresh shitake mushrooms, stems removed, sliced

½ lb fresh cremini mushrooms, stems removed, sliced

1 lb fresh "baby" Portobello mushrooms, stems removed, sliced

1 oz dried porcini mushrooms

3½ cups chicken broth

¼ cup tamari (wheat-free)

4 to 8 oz heavy cream, if desired

1. In a skillet over medium heat, cook the bacon pieces, stirring frequently, until the bacon is crisp. Remove the meat from the pan, placing it on a paper towel over a plate to absorb some of the fat.

2. Add the onion to the skillet and cook it in the fat and bacon bits in the pan, stirring until the onion starts to wilt, about 2 minutes. Add the sage and cayenne, and stir. Remove from heat.

3. Put the sliced fresh mushrooms in the slow cooker. Add the bacon and onion mix. Add the dried porcini, and top with the broth and tamari. Stir to combine. Cover and cook on Low for 5 to 6 hours or on High for about 3 hours.

4. If desired, stir in heavy cream, or ladle into bowls and pass the cream for those who want it.

The recipe calls for thick-cut bacon so that you get larger bacon pieces, but you can use any kind of bacon. Regular slices will yield smaller pieces. Smoked bacon will lend its flavor to the soup, as well, so if that's a flavor you like, try using that kind of bacon. You may want to skip the tamari if you choose smoked bacon.

Chicken Soup with Fennel and Escarole

The licorice flavor of fresh fennel is reinforced by fennel seeds in this easy and healthful Italian chicken soup.

Makes 6 to 8 servings.

1 lb boneless, skinless chicken breasts

1 large fennel bulb

3 tablespoons olive oil

2 large onions, diced

3 garlic cloves, minced

5 cups chicken stock or broth

14.5-oz can diced tomatoes, undrained

2 teaspoon fennel seeds, crushed

1 head escarole

Salt and pepper to taste

1. Rinse the chicken and pat dry with paper towels. Trim chicken of all visible fat, and cut into ½-inch cubes. Rinse the fennel and cut in half lengthwise. Discard core and ribs, and dice bulb into ¾-inch pieces. Place the chicken and fennel in the slow cooker.

2. Heat olive oil in a medium skillet over medium-high heat. Add onions and garlic and cook, stirring frequently, until onions are translucent, about 3 minutes. Scrape mixture into slow cooker.

3. Stir stock, tomatoes (with juice), and fennel seeds into the slow cooker and stir to combine all ingredients. Cover and cook on Low for 5 to 7 hours or on High for 2½ to 3 hours, or until chicken is cooked through and tender. While soup cooks, rinse escarole. Cut in half, discard core, and cut the remaining escarole into 1-inch strips.

4. If cooking on Low, raise the heat to High. Add escarole to the slow cooker and cook for an additional 30 to 40 minutes, or until the escarole is wilted. Season to taste with salt and pepper, and serve hot.

Fresh fennel, *finocchio* in Italian, and sometimes called *anise* in supermarkets, has a slightly licorice taste but the texture of celery, both raw and cooked. You can always substitute 2 celery ribs for each ½ fennel bulb specified in a recipe.

Spanish Seafood Stew

This is a heartier fish soup than most because it contains both smoky bacon and spicy chorizo sausage. I also love the nuances of orange in the broth.

Makes 4 to 6 servings.

½ lb thick cod fillet

½ lb swordfish fillet

½ lb bay scallops

2 juice oranges, washed

¼ lb bacon, cut into 1-inch pieces

1 medium onion, diced

1 carrot, sliced

1 celery rib, sliced

3 garlic cloves, minced

½ lb chorizo sausage, diced

14.5-oz can diced tomatoes, undrained

3½ cups seafood stock or fish broth

3 tablespoons chopped fresh basil

2 tablespoons chopped fresh parsley

1 tablespoon fresh thyme

1 bay leaf

Salt and pepper to taste

1. Rinse fish and pat dry with paper towels. Remove and discard any skin or bones. Cut fish into 1-inch cubes. Refrigerate fish and scallops until ready to use, covered with plastic wrap. Grate off orange zest, and then squeeze oranges for juice. Set aside.

2. Cook bacon in a heavy skillet over medium-high heat for 5 to 7 minutes, or until crisp. Remove bacon from the pan with a slotted spoon, and transfer it to the slow cooker. Discard all but 2 tablespoons of the bacon grease.

3. Add onions, carrot, celery, and garlic to the skillet and cook, stirring frequently, for about 3 minutes or until the onion is translucent. And the chorizo and cook for about 2 minutes more. Scrape mixture into the slow cooker.

4. Add tomatoes (with juice), orange zest, orange juice, stock, basil, parsley, thyme, and bay leaf to the slow cooker. Stir to combine. Cover and cook on Low for 6 to 8 hours or on High for 3 to 4 hours, or until vegetables are soft.

5. If cooking on Low, raise the heat to High. Add the fish and cook for another 30 to 50 minutes, or until it is cooked through and flakes easily. Remove and discard bay leaf. Season with salt and pepper, and serve.

> Chorizo is a pork sausage flavored with the Spanish spice pimenton, which is similar to paprika, and which gives it the characteristic dark red color. Depending on the type of pimenton used, the sausage is spicy or sweet, just as the more common Italian sausages are in the supermarket. Spicy chorizo is most commonly found in the United States and is best in this recipe.

Lobster Bisque

This elegant and indulgent bisque will impress your palette—and your guests!

Makes 4 to 6 servings.

2 whole lobsters, cooked

1 medium onion, quartered

1 stalk celery

1 bay leaf

½ cup water

2 tablespoons sherry wine

¼ teaspoon nutmeg

¼ teaspoon cayenne (optional)

Salt and freshly ground pepper

2 cups heavy cream

¼ cup fresh parsley, chopped

1. Using cooked lobsters, break up the lobster shells to remove the meat. Put the meat in a bowl and refrigerate until ready to use.

2. Put the shells in the slow cooker along with the onion, celery, and bay leaf. Pour the water and sherry over everything. Cover and cook on Low for 6 to 8 hours or on High for 3 to 4 hours.

3. When cooked, strain the broth through a sieve to remove all shells, vegetable chunks, and bay leaf. The strained broth should go in a large saucepan. Over low heat to keep it warm, add the nutmeg and cayenne (if desired), add the lobster meat, stir to combine, and season with salt and pepper.

4. Stir in the heavy cream and serve warm, garnishing with fresh parsley.

> If you're not going to serve the whole batch, put the soup in bowls before adding the cream, and add the cream as part of the garnish so it can be stirred in individually. The soup will store better without the cream in it. You can even freeze it.

Mmmm-Meatball Soup

The seasoning in the meatballs infuses the broth of the soup during cooking. The result is mm-mm-good!

Makes 4 to 6 servings.

1 lb ground turkey

½ onion, grated

1 carrot, grated

½ teaspoon dried thyme

¼ cup fresh parsley, chopped fine

1 large egg, lightly beaten

10 cups chicken stock or broth

4 cups Swiss chard, coarsely chopped

4 cups kale, coarsely chopped

Salt and pepper to taste

1. In a large bowl, combine ground turkey with onion, carrot, thyme, parsley, and egg. Wash your hands, and mix all the ingredients together with your hands (it's the best way—honestly!). Form meat mixture into meatballs and set aside.

2. Put the chicken broth in the slow cooker and carefully add the meatballs. Cover and cook on Low for 2 to 3 hours or on High for 1 to 2 hours, or until meatballs are cooked through.

3. If cooking on Low, increase the heat to High. Add the chopped greens, cover, and cook an additional 30 to 40 minutes or until greens are soft. Season with salt and pepper.

The chard and kale are hearty greens. You can substitute spinach or collard greens or do any combination of the greens that you'd like. If you choose to add just spinach, reduce the final cooking time to about 20 minutes, as spinach cooks faster than the others.

Back-for-More Beef Stew

Slow-cooked beef stew is such a treat. There's something about what happens to the vegetables when the fat and juices from the beef cook for hours alongside them that makes magic from simple ingredients.

Makes 4 to 6 servings.

2 tablespoons olive oil

1 onion, chopped fine

2 cloves garlic, minced

3 to 4 lbs chuck or bottom round beef

2 carrots, sliced

1 bunch Swiss chard, leaves and stems

1 turnip, peeled and cubed

4 cups beef stock or broth

1 teaspoon arrowroot for thickener, if desired

1. Heat the oil in a skillet and add the onions and garlic, cooking over medium-high heat until the onion is translucent, about 3 to 5 minutes.

2. Put the beef in the slow cooker and cover with the onion/garlic mixture. Add carrots, chard, and turnips, and pour beef broth over everything.

3. Cover and cook on Low for 6 to 8 hours or on High for 4 to 5 hours. If you like a thicker sauce, when the stew is cooked, take out about a half cup of the juices and mix in the arrowroot. Pour back into the stew and stir to combine. Let sit for 10 to 15 minutes on warm before serving.

> If you're in a real hurry, you can make this recipe with frozen vegetables, so long as they are low-carb, like broccoli, cauliflower, spinach, and blends.

Curried Broccoli Soup

So simple and so delicious, this is a soup you'll find yourself making over and over again.

Serves 4.

2 tablespoons unsalted butter

1 small onion, chopped

1 teaspoon curry powder

1 lb broccoli florets (tough stems removed)

1 teaspoon baking soda

3 cups chicken broth

Salt and pepper to taste

1. In a skillet over medium heat, cook the onion in the butter until translucent, 2 to 3 minutes. Remove from heat and stir in the curry powder.

2. Transfer the onion mixture to the slow cooker. Add the broccoli. Stir the baking soda into the chicken broth until dissolved, and pour over broccoli. Cover and cook on Low for 6 hours or on High for 4 hours.

3. Use a hand-held emulsifier to puree the soup, or process it in batches in a blender. Season with salt and pepper.

The addition of the baking soda will maintain the bright green color of the broccoli through the long cooking process.

Manhattan Clam Chowder

This tomato-based version of chowder has as many devoted fans as the creamy version has in New England. The combination of the vegetables and herbs in the base makes this recipe a real winner.

Makes 6 to 8 servings.

2 pints fresh minced clams

2 tablespoons olive oil

1 large onion, minced

2 celery ribs, diced

1 carrot, finely chopped

½ green bell pepper, seeds and ribs removed, chopped

28-oz can crushed tomatoes, undrained

Two 8-oz bottles clam juice

3 tablespoons chopped fresh parsley

1 tablespoon fresh thyme (½ teaspoon dried)

2 teaspoons fresh oregano (½ teaspoon dried)

2 bay leaves

Salt and pepper to taste

1. Drain clams, reserving juice. Refrigerate clams until ready to use.

2. Heat oil in a medium skillet over medium heat. Add onion, garlic, celery, carrot, and green pepper. Cook, stirring frequently, for about 5 minutes, or until onion is translucent. Scrape mixture into the slow cooker.

3. Add tomatoes (and juice), clam juice, juice drained from clams, parsley, thyme, oregano, and bay leaves to the slow cooker, and stir well. Cook on Low for 5 to 7 hours or on High for 2 to 3 hours, or until turnips are almost tender. If cooking on Low, raise the heat to High. Add clams, and continue cooking for an additional 30 minutes.

4. Remove and discard bay leaves, season to taste with salt and pepper, and serve hot.

It's now possible to find fresh minced clams in just about every supermarket. If they're not in the refrigerated case, check the freezer. Of course, the fresher the better, and if you can shop for your clams at a fish market or farmer's market, do so. Avoid canned clams.

Turkey-Veggie Stew

When I am at the end of a long week and have run out of time and energy for anything too creative, I turn to this super-simple recipe and know that all will be well at dinnertime.

Makes 4 to 6 servings.

1 tablespoon olive oil

1 onion, chopped

2 cloves garlic, minced

1 teaspoon ground cumin

1 lb ground turkey

16-oz package frozen broccoli

3 cups chicken or vegetable stock

Salt and pepper to taste

1. In a large skillet over medium-high heat, cook the onion and garlic in the olive oil for 3 to 4 minutes. Sprinkle the cumin over the mix, and continue stirring and cooking another minute or so.

2. Add ground turkey and cook until meat is browned, about 5 minutes.

3. Put mixture into the slow cooker. Top with the frozen broccoli and the stock. Cover and cook on Low for 5 to 6 hours or on High for 2 to 3 hours. Season with salt and pepper to taste.

This stew can be made more kid-friendly by making meatballs out of the turkey. Brown and cook them in the skillet before putting them in the slow cooker, and put the vegetables and broth around them.

Spring Sorrel Soup

Sorrel is a large herb that is harvested as a leafy vegetable. It has a distinct lemon-tart flavor that makes an excellent soup, especially with the addition of the coconut milk.

Makes 4 to 6 servings.

1 tablespoon olive oil

1 onion, chopped

4 cups fresh sorrel, stems removed and coarsely chopped

2 cups chicken broth

Salt and pepper to taste

8 ounces unsweetened almond milk, or to taste

1. Heat the olive oil in a skillet and add onions, cooking until translucent, about 5 minutes.

2. Put sorrel into the slow cooker, and add the chicken broth. Cover and cook on Low for 4 to 5 hours or on High for 2 to 3 hours. Season with salt and pepper to taste.

3. Remove a small cup and stir in some almond milk. If you like the flavor, add it to the rest of the soup. If you prefer the soup without it, leave it out.

You're not likely to find sorrel in the supermarket, but at a good farmer's market you should find it in the spring. It's easy to grow and is common across Europe. It is high in Vitamin C. The characteristic tartness is from the oxalic acid in the leaves, which is more pronounced in larger, older leaves. Younger leaves are great to put in salad.

Bouillabaisse

This is an amazing one-pot meal of assorted fish and shellfish that makes for a fun and festive meal on a summer night. If you've been really good on your low-carb diet, indulge in a low-carb bread to dip into the sauce.

Makes 6 to 8 servings.

1 onion, chopped

3 cloves garlic, minced

2 stalks celery, fronds removed, finely chopped

1 red pepper, seeded and chopped

8 oz fish stock (or clam juice)

½ cup water

2 tablespoons extra virgin olive oil

1 tablespoon lemon zest

1 tablespoon fresh basil, chopped

1 tablespoon fresh parsley, chopped

1 teaspoon fresh oregano

1 teaspoon fresh thyme

1 bay leaf

1 lb firm white fish, cut into 1-inch pieces

¾ lb shelled, cleaned shrimp, tails removed

6.5-oz can chopped clams and the juice

8 oz cleaned, fresh crabmeat

Salt to taste

¼ cup fresh parsley, chopped

1. In a large bowl, combine onions, garlic, celery, red pepper, fish stock, water, olive oil, zest, spices, and bay leaf. Mix well. Put into slow cooker.

2. Cover and cook on Low for 4 to 5 hours or on High for 2 to 3 hours until base is hot and flavors are combined.

3. Stir in fish, shrimp, clams, and crab and cook for an additional 45 minutes to 1 hour or until fish is done (if cooking on High, reduce heat to Low). Remove bay leaf before serving. Season with salt to taste and stir in or garnish with parsley.

This classic French fish "boil" is said to have originated in the seaside town of Marseilles in the south of France. The word itself has a fanciful attribution—bouille-besse, or the abbess' boil —in reference to a particular Abbesse in a convent there, as well as the more practical bouillon abaissé, meaning, "to reduce by evaporation."

Middle Eastern Spinach and Chicken Soup

The addition of turmeric to this simple soup adds a combination of color, flavor, and nutrition that's hard to beat.

Makes 6 to 8 servings.

4 tablespoons olive oil

3 cloves garlic, minced

½ pound boneless, skinless chicken breasts or tenders, cut into bite-sized cubes

2 teaspoons ground turmeric

16-oz package frozen chopped spinach

6 cups chicken stock

Salt and pepper to taste

Sriracha for garnishing, if desired

1. In a skillet over medium-high heat, cook the garlic in the oil until sizzling, about 3 minutes. Add the chicken pieces and stir, cooking until the pieces are white on all sides. Add the turmeric and stir to coat the chicken pieces. Remove from heat.

2. Transfer the meat to the slow cooker. Sprinkle with the frozen spinach, and add the chicken stock. Cover and cook on Low for 5 to 6 hours or on High for 3 to 4 hours.

3. Season with salt and pepper. Ladle into soup bowls and, if desired, make a small circle in the bowl with the Sriracha.

Want to use fresh spinach instead of frozen? You'll need a 10-ounce bag of baby spinach leaves, picked over and longer stems removed. Because it cooks so quickly—and you don't want to overcook it— wait until the soup has about 30 minutes more of cooking time in the slow cooker. Stir in the baby spinach leaves and cook for the remaining 20 to 30 minutes.

Creamed Cauliflower Soup

The nutty flavor of cauliflower shines through in this decadently creamy recipe. If you can find orange cauliflower, it not only has great color but contains about 25 percent more Vitamin A.

Makes 4 to 6 servings.

3 tablespoons olive oil

1 onion, chopped

2 cloves garlic, minced

1 head cauliflower, broken up into pieces, tough stem removed

2 cups chicken stock or broth

Salt and pepper to taste

8 ounces heavy cream or half-and-half

Fresh tarragon leaves for garnish

1. In a skillet over medium-high heat, cook the onions and garlic in the olive oil until onions are translucent, about 5 minutes. Scrape mixture into the slow cooker.

2. Put the cauliflower pieces in the slow cooker, and pour the chicken stock on top. Cover and cook on Low for 6 to 8 hours or on High for 4 to 5 hours.

3. Puree the soup with an immersion blender or by batches in a blender. Season with salt and freshly ground pepper.

4. Transfer to a serving pot, and stir in the cream or half-and-half. When serving, garnish with 4 or 5 fresh tarragon leaves.

Another option for a delicious and nutritious garnish is toasted almonds. To make them, preheat the oven to 350 degrees. On a cookie sheet, sprinkle sliced almonds. Cook them for 12 to 15 minutes, stirring every 4 to 5 minutes with a spatula until they are browned. Be careful not to overcook them. Transfer the cooked slices to a plate and allow to cool. Crumble or use whole.

Chunky Char-key Soup

This is a Swiss chard and turkey–based soup with a hint of nutmeg. Fragrant and filling, it's a low-carb take on Italian wedding soup. You won't miss the pasta, promise!

Makes 6 to 8 servings.

1 large bunch Swiss chard, ends trimmed, washed, and chopped

2 stalks celery, trimmed and diced

8 cups chicken stock

1 pound ground turkey

½ cup onion, minced fine

½ cup grated Parmesan cheese

Dash of nutmeg

2 tablespoons fresh parsley, chopped

1 egg, beaten

Salt and pepper to taste

1. Put the Swiss chard, celery, and chicken stock in the slow cooker. Cover and set to Low. Let the broth and vegetables cook while making the meatballs.

2. Combine the ground turkey, onion, cheese, nutmeg, parsley, and egg. Season with salt and pepper. Form into mini meatballs, setting them aside as you make them. When all the meat mixture is used up and the meatballs are formed, place them gently in the slow cooker.

3. Cover and cook on Low for 5 to 6 hours or on High for 4 hours, until the meatballs are cooked through. Serve with a garnish of fresh parsley.

Swiss chard is great for this soup because it has leaves and stems that can create different textures in the bowl. You can substitute kale, make it with a combination of these greens, or even supplement with dandelion greens if desired. If you want to use spinach, add fresh baby spinach greens in the last hour of cooking.

Tomato Soup

Make this soup when tomatoes are at their ripest—late summer—for the ultimate flavor. If you want a creamy soup, add some cream when pureeing the solids.

Makes 4 to 6 servings.

3 tablespoons olive oil

1 onion, diced

4 lbs ripe tomatoes, seeds removed and chopped

2 cups chicken stock or broth

½ teaspoon lemon juice

½ cup cream or half-and-half, if desired

Fresh dill, parsley, or basil for garnish

1. In a skillet over medium-high heat, add the oil and onion. Cook the onion until translucent, about 5 minutes. Scrape mixture into the slow cooker. Add the tomatoes and stock. Cover and cook on Low for 6 to 8 hours or on High for 4 to 5 hours.

2. When the soup is cooked, add the lemon juice. Puree the soup using an immersion blender. If you want to make the soup creamy, add the cream while you're pureeing it. Garnish with fresh dill, parsley, or basil.

Variations:

This is a simple and straightforward recipe—just the thing to use as a base for getting creative!

* Make the soup spicy by adding cayenne or even some sliced jalapenos in the cooking process.
* Give it a Middle Eastern taste by adding cumin or coriander (in which case you'll want to garnish with coriander).
* Make a hot gazpacho and top with diced pepper, onion, cucumber, and hard-boiled egg.

Low-Carb Beef and "Barley" Soup

On a cold day when you're just aching for a chewy grain, make a batch of this soup that uses quinoa instead of barley. While the carb count may be a bit high, quinoa is loaded with protein and fiber, two elements that make it an acceptable low-carb treat.

Makes 6 servings.

½ cup almond meal

½ teaspoon salt

1 teaspoon freshly ground black pepper

2 pounds beef stew meat, cut into bite-sized pieces

4 tablespoons olive oil

1 small onion, minced

10 oz fresh mushrooms, stemmed removed and caps quartered

3 stalks celery, chopped

2 teaspoons dried thyme

½ cup quinoa, rinsed

8 cups beef broth

Chopped fresh parsley for garnish

1. In a medium-sized bowl, combine almond meal with salt and pepper. Add the beef pieces and stir to coat. Remove the pieces, shaking off excess coating.

2. In a large skillet, heat 2 tablespoons of the olive oil. Add the beef pieces in batches, browning on all sides. Process in batches, transferring the pieces to a plate when browned. When all the pieces are cooked, add 2 more tablespoons of oil and add the onions, cooking and stirring up the browned bits of meat until the onions are translucent, about 3 minutes.

3. Add the mushrooms and celery, and continue to cook for 2 or 3 minutes. Stir in the thyme.

4. Transfer the onion mix to the slow cooker. Add the quinoa, and top with the beef. Pour the broth over all the ingredients. Cover and cook on Low for 6 to 7 hours or on High for 4 to 5 hours. Garnish with fresh parsley, if desired.

Quinoa has been grown in the Central and South American Andes for thousands of years. It's actually a seed, not a grain, and the leaves of the plant can be eaten, too. The seeds have a natural coating called a saponin that must be removed before eating. The seeds are loaded with protein, fiber, iron, magnesium, and phosphorous.

Shrimp and Vegetable Soup

This is a fun soup to make. It's a playful combination of vegetables and shrimp, with a nice dollop of dill.

Makes 4 servings.

1 carrot, peeled and sliced thin

2 cups broccoli florets, fresh or frozen

1 cup cauliflower florets, cubed

4 cups chicken stock

4 oz fresh baby spinach, stems removed, washed, and dried thoroughly

2 large egg yolks

½ lb shrimp, shelled and deveined

Salt and pepper to taste

2 tablespoons fresh dill, chopped (optional)

1. Into the slow cooker, add the carrot, broccoli, cauliflower, and stock. Cover and cook on High for 2 hours. Add the spinach, reduce heat to Low, and cook another hour.

2. In a small bowl, whisk the egg yolks until pale. Open the slow cooker and remove about 1 cup of the vegetable mixture into a measuring cup. Add gradually to the egg so that the hot mixture thickens. When thoroughly mixed, put this blend into the slow cooker with the rest, and stir to combine.

3. With the broth heated but not boiling, add the shrimp. Cover and cook until the shrimp are pink and just firm. Season to taste with salt and pepper. Serve, garnishing with dill if desired.

Variations:

✳ Substitute chopped red bell peppers for the cauliflower.

✳ Make the soup with Swiss chard instead of spinach.

✳ Saute some chorizo so that it's cooked through, and add it when you add the shrimp.

✳ Garnish with toasted sesame seeds instead of dill.

Earthy Watercress Soup

This soup is full of the earthy flavors of spring and summer—tangy yet delicate watercress, fresh mushrooms, and earthy tofu. Garnish with Parmesan crisps for extra deliciousness.

Makes 10 servings.

1 cup washed and shredded cabbage leaves

2 bunches watercress, washed, dried, and some stalk removed

1 small zucchini, cut into small pieces

2 large Portobello mushrooms, washed, patted dry, and chopped

8 cups chicken stock

2 cups water

4 tablespoons guar gum

2 scallions, white part only, sliced thin

1. Into the slow cooker, add the cabbage, watercress, zucchini, mushrooms, stock, and water. Cover and cook on Low for 3 to 4 hours or on High for 1 to 2 hours.

2. When liquid is bubbly and mushrooms are cooked through, stir in the guar gum and continue stirring with slow cooker on High for about 5 minutes until the liquid begins to thicken.

3. Use an immersion blender to puree the soup. Garnish with scallions, if desired.

To make Parmesan crisps to go with this soup, use fresh Parmesan. Grate 1 cup of the cheese. Preheat the oven to 350 degrees. Line a cookie sheet with parchment paper, and spray with non-stick cooking spray. Form circles of grated cheese on the sheet and bake for about 5 minutes. Keep an eye on them while they cook so they don't burn. Allow to cool before removing from the parchment.

Monkfish Moqueca

In Brazil, they make a spicy soup full of fresh fish, tomatoes, coconut, and spices. While monkfish is used in this recipe, any white-fleshed fish will do, as will shrimp or even calamari (or a combination). The flavors make for a fiesta in your mouth.

Makes 6 to 8 servings.

2 tablespoons olive oil

½ onion, minced

2 cloves garlic, minced

¼ cup roasted red peppers, chopped

14-oz can diced tomatoes

1 cup coconut milk

1½ to 2 lbs monkfish, cut into chunks

¼ cup fresh cilantro, chopped

2 tablespoons Sriracha hot sauce

2 tablespoons fresh-squeezed lime juice

Salt and pepper to taste

1. In a skillet over medium-high heat, cook the onion and garlic in the olive oil until onion is translucent, about 3 minutes. Add the roasted red peppers and stir.

2. Transfer the mixture to the slow cooker. Add the diced tomatoes and coconut milk. Cover and cook on Low for 4 to 5 hours or on High for 2 to 3 hours.

3. Add the monkfish and cilantro. Cover and continue to cook on Low for 30 to 45 minutes or until the fish is cooked through.

4. Stir in the Sriracha and fresh-squeezed lime juice. Season with salt and pepper. Garnish with additional chopped cilantro if desired.

When you eat a dish full of so much flavor, you really don't need the carbs that pasta or potatoes contribute. This tastes so good that you'll want more than one bowl.

Chapter 4

Beef, Pork, and Lamb Dishes

*M*eat is a staple of the low-carb lifestyle and is a joy to cook in the slow cooker. Tougher cuts can be cooked to tender perfection, meats can be the stars of a great number of delicious stews, and you can craft delicious meals without the heat from the oven or the sometimes overpowering smell of meat cooking (which can often be a wonderful thing, like the turkey cooking on Thanksgiving, but can also be torturous if you're trying to diet!). The recipes in this chapter feature beef, pork, and lamb--everything from a classic meat loaf to curry stew, roasts, and ribs. There are dishes that can be slow-cooked and then finished on the grill. And there are dishes that can be ready for a fancy dinner party, leaving you time to tend to other things. Finally, there are lots of ideas for how to vary the dishes, so have fun with them and let the slow cooker work its magic.

Bacon-Wrapped Meat Loaf

This is a fun dish to make in the slow cooker. The juices will seep out and form their own sauce, so you won't need ketchup—just spoon the juices over the meat when serving.

Makes 6 to 8 servings.

8-oz can tomato sauce (or tomatoes with chili peppers if you want to add some zing)

3 eggs, beaten

1 lb ground pork

1 lb ground veal

2 slices low-carb bread, crusts removed, broken into small pieces

½ cup grated Parmesan cheese

½ onion, chopped fine

2 cloves garlic, minced

1 tablespoon chopped fresh parsley

1 teaspoon kosher or sea salt

1 teaspoon coarsely ground black pepper

4 slices bacon

1. In a large mixing bowl, combine tomato sauce, eggs, meats, bread pieces, cheese, onion, garlic, and parsley. Wash your hands, and use them to stir the mixture. Season with salt and pepper. Form into a brick shape that will fit nicely in the slow cooker.

2. Cook the bacon in the microwave for a few minutes until just cooked. Wrap it over the loaf, tucking the ends under. Place the loaf in the slow cooker. Cover and cook on Low for 7 to 8 hours, or on High for 5 to 6 hours.

In this recipe I've opted for the low-carb bread slices to act as the filler in the meatloaf. There are other ingredients that can do this, too. Spinach or green peppers will add some density, but you'll get a lot of juice. The bread is really the best for absorbing the juices and keeping the meat moist.

Pork Chops with Sauerkraut

This is another one of those meals where you're going to be so pleased with the result that you will want to make it once a week in the fall or winter.

Makes 2 to 4 servings.

1 to 2 lbs boneless pork chops (3 or 4)

½ teaspoon thyme

Salt and freshly ground pepper

1 package (16 oz) sauerkraut

3 or 4 slices from a large red onion, sliced thin

1 teaspoon caraway seeds

½ teaspoon mustard seed

½ cup dry white wine

¼ cup heavy cream, if desired

Fresh parsley for garnish

1. Put pork chops on a plate and sprinkle both sides with thyme, salt, and pepper.

2. Put the sauerkraut in the slow cooker, spread the onions over it, and top with caraway and mustard seeds.

3. Heat oil in a skillet over medium heat. Brown the chops in 2 tablespoons oil turning to brown on both sides.

4. Transfer the chops to the slow cooker, and top with white wine. Cover and cook on Low for 6 to 8 hours or on High for 4 to 5 hours.

5. Before serving, transfer chops to a plate and cover to keep warm. Stir cream into sauerkraut, if desired. Divide kraut between plates and top with chops. Garnish with fresh parsley.

Sauerkraut means "sour cabbage," and the sourness comes from the lactic fermentation of the vegetable's sugars. A version of sauerkraut exists in countries around the world, as the fermentation led to a long shelf life. It's a dish that's often served with bacon, sausage, and other cuts of pork.

Plentiful Peppers and Beef in Lettuce Wraps

Make this dish for a late lunch, early dinner, or appetizer for a football party. It's a great low-carb finger food.

Makes 8 to 10 servings.

¼ cup olive oil

1 small onion, chopped

2 each of medium-sized yellow, red, and orange bell peppers, cored, seeded and sliced

4.5-oz can chopped green chili peppers

1 teaspoon ancho chili powder

2 to 3 lbs sirloin beef, cut into thin strips

2 28-oz cans tomato puree

1 head crisp lettuce greens, like Romaine or endive, cut or broken into 3-inch sections

Grated cheddar or Pepperjack cheese for garnish

1. Heat the oil in a large skillet or saucepan. Add the onion and peppers and cook until just softening, about 5 minutes. Stir in the green chili peppers and ancho chili powder.

2. Transfer pepper mixture to the slow cooker. Top with the slices of steak, and pour the tomato puree over everything. Cover and cook on Low for 6 to 8 hours, or on High for 5 to 6 hours until the steak is tender.

3. To serve, put the steak and pepper mix in a bowl with a lid, and serve alongside a platter of prepared lettuce leaves. Fill the leaves as necessary so they don't get soggy and tear. Sprinkle grated cheese on top.

If you want to wrap the peppers and beef in something besides lettuce leaves, consider low-carb tortillas. For extra tastiness, brush them on both sides with some olive oil and toast them on the grill for a minute or so a side.

Southwest Pulled Beef

Using jarred salsa and a variety of spices to flavor the beef chunks in this recipe yields a pungent, tender "pulled beef" dish that's delicious in an assortment of veggie cups—cherry tomatoes, hollowed cucumbers, or peppers.

Makes 6 or more servings.

2 tablespoons olive oil

1 teaspoon ground cumin

½ teaspoon dried oregano

½ teaspoon cayenne pepper

½ teaspoon ancho chili powder

2 to 3 lbs chuck roast

2 16-oz jars or 1 32-oz jar salsa, no sugar added

½ cup fresh-squeezed lime juice

8-oz can tomato puree

1. In a medium-sized bowl, combine the oil, cumin, oregano, cayenne pepper, and ancho chili powder. Whisk to combine. Put the meat in the marinade, allowing to sit 30 minutes or so, turning about every 10 minutes.

2. Heat a large skillet and pour in some of the seasoned oil. Brown the meat on both sides. Transfer to the slow cooker. Discard the excess oil.

3. Pour the salsa, lime juice, and tomato puree on the meat. Cover and cook on Low for 6 to 8 hours, or on High for about 5 hours.

> Indulge in a dollop of sour cream with this dish. It's the perfect low-carb complement.

Venison Stew

Venison is deer meat, and if you live where deer are plentiful and you know some hunters, you can get a supply from them. The meat is much leaner than beef, perfect for stews. This is the kind of meal you want to make on a long winter's night. It's rich and delicious.

Makes 6 to 8 servings.

4-pound venison shoulder

Salt and pepper to taste

4 to 6 slices bacon

¼ cup bacon drippings

2 onions, diced

1 stalk celery, diced

¼ cup almond flour

12-oz can diced tomatoes

½ cup mushrooms, sliced

2 cloves garlic, crushed

3 cups beef stock or broth

1 cup red wine

1 sprig fresh thyme

1 sprig fresh rosemary

2 bay leaves

1. Season the venison with salt and pepper. In a heavy-bottomed skillet, cook the bacon, reserving the cooked strips. In the bacon drippings, cook the venison so that it is browned on all sides. Put the venison in the slow cooker.

2. Into the skillet add the onions and celery, and stir frequently until they have browned slightly. Add the almond flour and stir to combine. Put the mixture into the slow cooker with the venison.

3. In a large bowl, combine the tomatoes, mushrooms, garlic, beef stock, red wine, thyme, rosemary, and bay leaves. Pour this over and around the venison. Cook on Low for 6 to 8 hours or on High for 5 to 7 hours.

> Venison is rich in B vitamins, iron, and phosphorous but low in fat and cholesterol.

Short Ribs with Adobo

Adobo is the Spanish word for "marinade," and throughout the Caribbean, the Central and South Americas, and in the Phillipines, adobo sauces are commonly used with meats. They vary, of course, depending on the country and the meat. This one is composed to complement the delectable flavor of the short ribs of beef.

Makes 4 to 6 servings.

2 tablespoons olive oil

4 lbs short ribs, bone in, excess fat trimmed

Salt and pepper

2 tablespoons Spanish paprika (sweet or spicy)

2 tablespoons dried oregano

3 large garlic cloves, minced

4 tablespoons cider vinegar

1 teaspoon red chili paste (if desired)

1. Heat oil in large skillet, season ribs with salt and pepper, and brown the ribs on both sides. Transfer to the slow cooker.

2. In a medium bowl, combine the oil from the skillet, paprika, oregano, garlic, vinegar, and (if you want real heat) the chili paste. Stir to mix well.

3. Pour or scoop the mixture over the short ribs. Cover and cook on Low for 8 to 10 hours or on High for 4 to 5 hours.

To complement the Caribbean flavors in this dish, serve the ribs with cauliflower "rice" and fried eggplant slices to replace fried plantains.

Balsamic-Sage Chops

This is an easy recipe to put together, and it's universally enjoyed.

Makes 6 servings.

4 tablespoons olive oil

6 boneless pork chops

1 large sweet onion, cut into thin slices

1 teaspoon dried sage

Salt and freshly ground pepper

¼ cup balsamic vinegar

¼ cup chicken stock

1. Heat the oil in a large skillet. Brown the chops in the hot oil on both sides. Transfer to slow cooker.

2. Add onions to skillet and cook, stirring, until just translucent, 2 or so minutes. Transfer to the slow cooker.

3. Sprinkle the chops and onions with the sage, season with salt and pepper, and add the balsamic and chicken stock. Cover and cook on Low for 6 to 8 hours or on High for 3 to 4 hours.

A touch of sweetness can really enliven this dish, so I sometimes experiment by adding a tablespoon of maple syrup or raw honey to the balsamic before adding to the slow cooker.

Lamb with Mint Pesto

Make the simple roast in the slow cooker, and serve it warm with the mint pesto. This is also delicious sliced thin and served on pieces of endive as an elegant lunch or appetizer.

Makes 4 to 6 servings.

4-lb leg of lamb, deboned and wrapped in kitchen twine

2 cloves garlic, cut into slivers

1 tablespoon olive oil

1 tablespoon dried rosemary

½ teaspoon salt

1 teaspoon freshly ground pepper

2 cups dry red wine

PESTO

1 cup packed fresh mint leaves (no stalks)

4 cloves garlic

¼ cup olive oil

¼ cup toasted pepitos (pumpkin seeds)

Salt to taste

1. Prepare the lamb by studding with the garlic slivers (poke a sharp knife into the flesh and insert a sliver) all around the roast. Put the olive oil on your hands and cover the roast with the olive oil. Place it in the slow cooker. Add the rosemary, salt, pepper, and wine.

2. Cover and cook on Low for 8 to 10 hours or on High for 5 to 6 hours, until meat is tender.

3. While the lamb is cooking, prepare the pesto. Put the mint, garlic, olive oil, and pepitos in a blender or food processor, and pulse until ingredients are thoroughly blended. Scrape into a bowl, season with some salt, cover with plastic wrap and store in the refrigerator until ready to serve.

Pesto is traditionally made with basil, pine nuts, olive oil, garlic, and Parmesan cheese, but you can vary the ingredients in many ways, substituting other herbs for the basil and other nuts for the pine nuts, and skipping the cheese altogether. You're limited to low-carb nuts on this diet, but those include pumpkin seeds, sunflower seeds, almonds, and hazelnuts.

Meat Sauce

There's a great assortment of vegetables in this sauce, all slow-cooked with the meat, to give the appearance of a really meaty sauce. Kids love it!

Makes 8 to 10 servings.

2 tablespoons olive oil

1 onion, chopped fine

2 small zucchini, chopped

1 green bell pepper, seeds and ribs removed, chopped fine

8 oz button mushrooms, rinsed and sliced thick

1 lb ground beef

1 lb ground turkey

2 lbs ripe tomatoes, seeds removed and chopped

2 14.5-oz cans diced tomatoes, undrained

3 cloves garlic, minced

2 teaspoon dried oregano

1 tablespoon dried basil

1 teaspoon red pepper flakes

Salt and pepper to taste

1. In a large skillet over medium-high heat, add the olive oil, onion, zucchini, pepper, and mushrooms. Cook, stirring, for about 3 minutes, and put in the bottom of the slow cooker.

2. In the same skillet, brown the ground meats together over medium heat, being careful not to cook too long. The meat should be slightly pink. Put it in the slow cooker on top of the vegetables.

3. Add both types of tomatoes, garlic, oregano, basil, and red pepper flakes. Stir to combine. Cover and cook on Low for 4 to 6 hours or on High for about 2 hours. Season with salt and pepper.

While you can't eat regular pasta on a low-carb diet, you can make a delightful bowl of spaghetti squash upon which to serve this sauce. You can also slice long zucchini with a mandoline to make "noodles." When you have been on the low-carb diet for a while, you can experiment with low-carb pastas, but they must be eaten only on occasion. Lots of other foods are great with spaghetti sauce!

Spicy Spareribs

These are so tasty when they come out of the slow cooker that you'll want to eat them right away. But to make them extra-special, finish them on a hot grill, allowing just a couple of minutes per side to give them a crunchy outside.

Makes 4 to 6 servings.

2 tablespoons olive oil

3 lbs country-style spareribs (thick cut)

1 teaspoon cayenne pepper

Salt and freshly ground pepper

28-oz can crushed tomatoes, with juice

1 teaspoon cumin

½ teaspoon cinnamon

½ teaspoon ancho chili powder

½ teaspoon garlic powder

1. Put the olive oil in a baking dish. Put the ribs in the dish and stir and toss them to coat with olive oil. Sprinkle the oiled ribs with cayenne, salt, and pepper. Place in the slow cooker.

2. In a bowl, combine the crushed tomatoes, cumin, cinnamon, ancho chili powder, and garlic powder. Stir. Pour over ribs. Cover and cook on Low for 8 to 10 hours.

3. Skim fat off the top, finish the ribs on the grill if you want them crunchy on the outside, and serve the sauce on the side.

As you make the spicy sauce with the crushed tomatoes, taste it and consider varying the flavor by using more or less of the listed spices, and even adding something else you like. If you want something a bit less smoky, substitute red pepper flakes for the ancho chili powder. A word of caution, though: Don't overdo the cinnamon.

Pot Roast with Mushrooms in Truffle Oil

The combination of fresh and dried mushrooms adds so much earthy flavor to this dish! Savor every bite.

Makes 6 to 8 servings.

4 to 5 lbs chuck roast

4 tablespoons herb-infused olive oil (see sidebar)

2 cloves garlic, minced

1 lb fresh white mushrooms, sliced

½ lb "babybellas"—small Portobello mushrooms, stems removed

¼ lb dried shitaki mushrooms

2 cups beef broth

Salt and pepper

½ cup sour cream (if desired)

1. Place roast in the slow cooker.

2. Heat oil in a skillet over medium heat. Add garlic and both types of fresh mushrooms. Stir and cook until mushrooms soften, about 5 minutes. Remove from heat and add the dried mushrooms.

3. Transfer the mushroom mixture to the slow cooker. Top with the beef broth. Cover and cook on Low for 8 to 10 hours or on High for 6 to 8 hours. Season with salt and pepper.

4. If desired, stir in sour cream just before serving.

Cooking the mushrooms in an herb-infused olive oil can bring out their earthiness even more. Try popular types like basil/garlic, or pepper/garlic. If you don't have any handy, just go with extra virgin olive oil and add a teaspoon of sage after cooking the mushrooms.

Lamb Stew with Prosciutto and Bell Peppers

Lamb is an inherently rich meat, and the sweetness of red bell peppers combined with bits of salty prosciutto serve as perfect foils to that richness.

Makes 4 to 6 servings.

½ cup almond flour

2 lbs boneless lamb shoulder or leg of lamb, fat trimmed and cut into cubes

¼ cup olive oil

1 onion, diced

3 cloves garlic, minced

¼ lb prosciutto, cut into ½-inch chunks

1 cup dry red wine

1 cup beef stock or broth

2 tablespoons fresh sage, chopped

2 tablespoons fresh parsley, chopped

2 tablespoons fresh rosemary, chopped

1 large red bell pepper, seeds and ribs removed, thinly sliced

Salt and pepper to taste

1. Put almond flour in a large bowl and add meat, stirring to coat.

2. Heat oil in a large skillet and add meat pieces, shaking off excess flour as you transfer them from the bowl to the skillet. Brown the meat on all sides. Use a slotted spoon to put browned pieces in the slow cooker.

3. Add onion, garlic, and prosciutto to the skillet and cook, stirring, for about 3 minutes. Scrape this onto the meat in the slow cooker.

4. Add wine to the skillet, and bring to a boil, stirring to dislodge the brown bits in the skillet. Pour mixture into the slow cooker. Add stock, sage, parsley, and rosemary to the slow cooker, and stir well. Cook on Low for 6 to 8 hours or on High for 3 to 4 hours, or until lamb is almost tender.

5. If cooking on Low, raise heat to High. Add peppers, and cook for about an hour longer, or until lamb is tender. Season with salt and pepper.

> Lamb is one of those meats that people either love or don't care for. If your family members are mixed on their taste for lamb, prepare this stew without telling them what kind of meat is featured. I'll bet everyone enjoys it thoroughly!

Short Ribs of Beef with Rosemary and Fennel

Short ribs are a wonderful cut because they become so meltingly tender when slowly braised in the slow cooker. The aromatic rosemary in the simple sauce cuts through the richness of the meat well.

Makes 4 to 6 servings.

5 lbs meaty short ribs with bones

¼ cup olive oil

1 large onion, minced

4 cloves garlic, sliced

2 cups beef stock or broth

1 large fennel bulb, cored, trimmed, and sliced

2 tablespoons fresh parsley, chopped

2 tablespoons fresh rosemary

2 teaspoons arrowroot

Salt and pepper to taste

1. Preheat the oven broiler, and line a broiler pan with heavy-duty aluminum foil. Broil short ribs for 3 to 4 minutes per side, or until browned. Arrange short ribs in the slow cooker, and pour in any juices that have collected in the pan.

2. Heat oil in a medium skillet over medium-high heat. Add onion and garlic, and cook, stirring frequently, for 3 minutes, or until onion is translucent. Scrape mixture into the slow cooker. Add stock, fennel, parsley, and rosemary to the slow cooker, and stir well.

3. Cook on Low for 8 to 10 hours or on High for 4 to 5 hours, or until short ribs are very tender. Remove as much grease as possible from the slow cooker with a soup ladle.

4. If cooking on Low, raise the heat to High. Mix arrowroot with 2 tablespoons cold water in a small cup. Stir this mixture into the cooker, and cook on High for 15 to 20 minutes, or until juices are bubbling and slightly thickened. Season with salt and pepper.

> Our English word for beef comes from the Latin *bos*, which means "ox." By the Middle Ages, it had become *boef* or *beef* in English. There were cattle at the Jamestown settlement in Virginia in the early seventeenth century, but the Texas longhorns that we use for beef today were brought to that state by the Spanish almost a century after the Jamestown settlement.

Beef Stew with Paprika

Paprika adds a wonderful smokiness to this dish that is Hungarian in origin.

Makes 4 to 6 servings.

½ cup almond flour

2 lbs stew meat, fat trimmed and cut into cubes

3 tablespoons olive oil

1 large onion, diced

3 cloves garlic, minced

2 tablespoons sweet paprika

2 teaspoons ground cumin

1 cup dry red wine

1 cup beef stock or broth

14.5-oz can diced tomatoes, undrained

2 tablespoons fresh parsley, chopped

2 tablespoons fresh rosemary, chopped

1 bay leaf

Salt and pepper to taste

1. Put almond flour in a large bowl and add meat, stirring to coat.

2. Heat oil in a large skillet and add meat pieces, shaking off excess flour as you transfer them from the bowl to the skillet. Brown the meat on all sides. Use a slotted spoon to put browned pieces in the slow cooker.

3. Add onion and garlic to the skillet and cook, stirring, for about 3 minutes. Add paprika and cumin and cook for 1 minute, stirring constantly. Scrape this onto the meat in the slow cooker.

4. Add wine to the skillet, and bring to a boil, stirring to dislodge the brown bits in the skillet. Pour mixture into the slow cooker.

5. Add stock, tomatoes, parsley, rosemary, and bay leaf to the slow cooker, and stir well. Cook on Low for 8 to 10 hours or on High for 4 to 5 hours, or until beef is tender. Remove and discard bay leaf. Season with salt and pepper.

An easy way to coat food with flour is to place the flour and food in a heavy plastic bag. Keep the air in the bag so the food can move around freely, and hold the top tightly closed with your hand. Shake the food around, and it will be evenly coated.

Perfect Pot Roast

This tender and flavorful roast is as good on a summer night as it is in the heart of winter, because the slow cooker doesn't heat the whole kitchen.

Makes 4 to 6 servings.

2- to 3-lb boneless chuck or rump roast

3 tablespoons olive oil

1 large onion, diced

4 cloves garlic, minced

2 cups beef stock or broth

4 ribs celery, trimmed and cut into slices

1 turnip, cut into small cubes

2 tablespoons fresh rosemary, chopped

2 tablespoons fresh parsley, chopped

1 teaspoon fresh thyme, chopped

1½ tablespoons arrowroot

Salt and pepper to taste

1. Preheat the oven broiler, and line a broiler pan with heavy-duty aluminum foil. Broil beef for 3 to 4 minutes per side, or until browned. Transfer beef to the slow cooker, and pour in any juices that have collected in the pan.

2. Heat oil in a medium skillet over medium-high heat. Add onion and garlic and cook, stirring frequently, for 3 minutes, or until onion is translucent. Scrape mixture into the slow cooker.

3. Add stock, celery, turnip, rosemary, parsley, and thyme to the slow cooker, and stir well. Cook on Low for 8 to 10 hours or on High for 4 to 5 hours, or until beef is very tender. Remove as much grease as possible from the slow cooker with a soup ladle or baster.

4. If cooking on Low, raise the heat to High. Mix arrowroot with 2 tablespoons cold water in a small cup, and stir it into the slow cooker. Cook on High for 15 to 20 minutes, or until juices are bubbling and slightly thickened.

5. Remove roast from the slow cooker. Season to taste with salt and pepper. Slice it against the grain into thin slices and serve the vegetables and juices on the side. Garnish with some additional parsley if desired.

Unlike most other roasted meats, braised dishes don't need time to "rest" for the juices to be reabsorbed into the fibers of the meat. With this pot roast, the juices from the meat are integrated into the sauce, which then moistens the meat.

Peppered Pork Tenderloin

A pork tenderloin is a blank canvas. There are so many ways you can prepare it—all very low-carb or even no carb! Here's a recipe that yields a tender and tangy meal. Serve with a mild vegetable, like steamed broccoli.

Serves 4.

1 whole pork tenderloin, about 1 pound

2 teaspoons no-salt, no-MSG lemon pepper seasoning

½ teaspoon cayenne (red pepper) or pepper blend seasoning

¼ cup chicken stock

1. Rub tenderloin with both pepper seasonings, covering entire surface.

2. Place in the slow cooker and spread the stock around the sides. Cover and cook on Low for 4 to 6 hours, or on High for 2 to 3 hours, until meat is cooked through and tender.

3. Let roast rest for 5 minutes before slicing to serve.

A word of caution about pork tenderloins. They are often sold in a marinade, such as teriyaki, lemon garlic, mesquite, and so on. The marinades are typically loaded with salt and artificial ingredients, so while they may look and sound tempting, a pork tenderloin is such a nice cut of meat that can be so easily seasoned with fresh herbs and spices that there's no need to buy the pre-marinated packages.

Barbecued Smoked Pork

Searing meats over aromatic woods on the grill, and then giving them time in the slow cooker, you can replicate the wonderful heady flavor and falling apart tenderness of traditional barbecue. I deferred to the Atkins community for this recipe for barbeque sauce. It is full of flavor with no sugar, and you can customize it by adding more or less of the spices listed to suit your taste.

Makes 4 to 6 servings.

1½ cups hickory or mesquite chips

2½-lb boneless pork shoulder

2 cloves garlic, crushed

Salt and pepper to taste

1½ cups chicken stock or broth

1 cup low-carb BBQ sauce

BARBECUE SAUCE

1 tablespoon virgin olive oil

4 tablespoons finely chopped onion

2 tablespoons tomato paste

1 teaspoon chili powder

1 teaspoon ground cumin

¾ teaspoon garlic powder

¾ teaspoon ground mustard seed

¼ teaspoon ground allspice

⅛ teaspoon cayenne pepper

1½ cups no-added-sugar ketchup

1 tablespoon cider vinegar

2 teaspoons Worcestershire sauce

¼ teaspoon instant coffee granules

1. If using a charcoal grill, soak the chips in water for at least 30 minutes. If using a gas grill, place the dry chips in a 12x18-inch piece of heavy-duty aluminum foil. Bring up the foil on all sides, and roll the ends together to seal the packet. Poke several small holes in the top of the packet.

2. Rub pork with garlic, salt, and pepper. Drain the wood chips, and sprinkle chips on the hot coals, or place packet over preheated grid. Place pork on the grill rack and close the grill's lid, or cover it with a sheet of heavy-duty aluminum foil. Smoke pork for 10 minutes per side, turning it with tongs.

3. Place pork in the slow cooker and add stock. Cook pork for 8 to 10 hours on Low or on High for 4 to 5 hours, or until meat is very tender. Season to taste with salt and pepper.

4. To make the barbecue sauce: Heat oil in a medium saucepan over medium-high heat. Add onion and sauté until soft, about 3 minutes. Add tomato paste, chili powder, cumin, garlic powder, mustard seed, allspice, and cayenne pepper, and cook until fragrant, about 1 minute. Stir in ketchup, vinegar, Worcestershire sauce, and coffee; simmer, stirring occasionally, until very thick, about 8 minutes. Serve warm or at room temperature, or refrigerate in an airtight container for up to 3 days.

5. Remove pork from the slow cooker, and slice it against the grain into thin slices. Spoon some pan juices over meat, and pass barbecue sauce separately.

Bouef Bourguignon

Simple, elegant, and classic, this is the "stew" you make for special occasions. It's irresistible.
Vive la France!

Makes 2 to 4 servings.

2 lbs stewing beef, fat trimmed, and cut into cubes

2 tablespoons olive oil

1 large onion, diced

3 cloves garlic, minced

½ lb white mushrooms, rinsed, stemmed, and sliced thick

1½ cups dry red wine

1 cup beef stock (use real stock for this; it adds a whole other dimension)

1 tablespoon tomato paste

1 teaspoon herbes de Provence

3 tablespoons fresh parsley, chopped

1 bay leaf

1½ tablespoons arrowroot

Salt and pepper to taste

1. Preheat the oven broiler, and line a broiler pan with heavy-duty aluminum foil. Broil beef cubes for 3 minutes per side, or until browned. Transfer cubes to the slow cooker, and pour in any juices that have collected in the pan.

2. Heat oil in a medium skillet over medium-high heat. Add onion, garlic, and mushrooms, and cook, stirring frequently, for 4 to 5 minutes, or until onion is translucent and mushrooms are soft. Scrape mixture into the slow cooker.

3. Add wine, stock, tomato paste, herbes de Provence, parsley, and bay leaf to the slow cooker, and stir well. Cook on Low for 8 to 10 hours or on High for 4 to 5 hours, or until beef is very tender.

4. If cooking on Low, raise the heat to High. Mix arrowroot with 2 tablespoons cold water in a small cup, and stir it into the slow cooker. Cook on High for 15 to 20 minutes, or until juices are bubbling and slightly thickened. Remove and discard bay leaf, and season to taste with salt and pepper. Garnish with some additional parsley if desired.

Many stew recipes call for wine, and most typically a nice, dry red. Fortunately, these are the wines with the lowest rates of residual sugar (and sugar is what you want to avoid), so they're safe to use, especially in the quantities required. Since you won't be using much, a great thing to do is pour the rest of the bottle into ice cube trays and freeze it. When you need the wine for another recipe, simply pull out a few cubes and thaw.

Pork Stew with Curry

This easy-to-prepare meal is a refreshing change from more traditionally American preparations.

Makes 6 to 8 servings.

1 lb boneless pork loin, cubed

2 tablespoons olive oil

1 onion, chopped

1 clove garlic, minced

2 tablespoons curry powder

2 turnips, cubed

16-oz can diced tomatoes

½ cup apple cider vinegar

½ head cauliflower florets

1. Heat oil in skillet and add pork cubes, stirring to brown on all sides. Move the pork cubes to the slow cooker. Cook onions in the remaining oil in the skillet until translucent, about 3 minutes. Add the garlic and stir for another minute.

2. Remove from heat and stir in the curry and turnips. Stir to coat. Add the turnip and spice mix to the slow cooker. Add the tomatoes and vinegar.

3. Cover and cook on Low for 7 to 8 hours or on High for 4 to 5 hours, until the meat is very tender. In the last hour of cooking, add the cauliflower florets (so they don't overcook).

Variation:

✳ For a spicier curry, add a ½ teaspoon each of cumin and cayenne pepper.

Prime Rib

Yes, it is possible to make an amazing prime rib in the slow cooker! Searing the meat before it goes into the slow cooker is the key.

Makes 6 to 8 servings.

6- to 8-lb rib roast
4 tablespoons olive oil
Salt and pepper to taste
Meat thermometer

1. Trim excess fat from the roast.

2. In a large, heavy bottomed skillet, heat the oil until sizzling. Place the roast, fat side down, onto the oil and allow to cook until browned, 3 to 4 minutes. Turn the roast to the side and do the same, then flip it to brown the other side. Turn off the skillet.

3. Place the roast in the slow cooker. Season with generous sprinkling of freshly ground black pepper and kosher or sea salt. Cover and cook on Low for 6 hours.

4. Check the internal temperature of the meat by inserting the thermometer into a meaty section between some ribs. For medium, the temperature should read about 145 degrees. If it's at that temperature or 5 to 10 degrees below, take it out of the slow cooker and let it rest on a warm plate. It can rest uncovered for 15 to 30 minutes.

> Isn't it a great feeling when you have done so little to prepare a dish, and yet it turns out so beautifully and is so delicious? I know it is for me!

Pork Provençal

This vibrant stew punctuated with olives contains many of the flavors common to dishes from this sunny part of southern France, including red bell peppers and leeks.

Makes 4 servings.

1½ lbs boneless pork loin, cut into cubes

4 leeks, white parts only

2 tablespoons olive oil

4 cloves garlic, minced

2 red bell peppers, seeds and ribs removed, and thinly sliced

14.5-oz can diced tomatoes, drained

1 cup dry red wine

1 cup chicken stock or broth

¾ cup pitted oil-cured black or green olives

1 tablespoon herbes de Provence

3 tablespoons fresh parsley, chopped

1 bay leaf

1 tablespoon arrowroot

Salt and pepper to taste

1. Preheat the oven broiler, and line a broiler pan with heavy-duty aluminum foil. Broil pork for 3 minutes per side, or until browned. Transfer cubes to the slow cooker, and pour in any juices that have collected in the pan.

2. Trim leeks, split lengthwise, and slice thinly. Place slices in a colander and rinse well under cold running water, rubbing with your fingers to dislodge all dirt. Shake leeks in the colander.

3. Heat oil in a medium skillet over medium-high heat. Add leeks, garlic, and red peppers, and cook, stirring frequently, for 3 minutes, or until leeks are translucent. Scrape mixture into the slow cooker.

4. Add tomatoes, wine, stock, olives, herbes de Provence, parsley, and bay leaf to the slow cooker, and stir well. Cook on Low for 6 to 8 hours or on High for 3 to 4 hours, or until pork is tender.

5. If cooking on Low, raise the heat to High. Mix arrowroot with 2 tablespoons cold water in a small cup, and stir it into the slow cooker. Cook on High for 15 to 20 minutes, or until juices are bubbling and slightly thickened. Remove and discard bay leaf, and season to taste with salt and pepper.

Oil-cured black olives are olives that have been dried and are then macerated in oil for several months. This allows them to last without needing a liquid brine. They are sometimes offered with additional seasonings, like hot pepper flakes. For this recipe, go for the plain version. They are delicious. Double-check for pits just to be on the safe side.

Lazy Lady's Leg of Lamb

Don't you just love the name of this recipe? You'll love the dish even more—promise! It's so delicious, and always comes out just right, with no fuss!

Makes 6 to 8 servings.

1 bone-in leg of lamb (shank removed)

1 tablespoon olive oil

½ teaspoon sea salt

½ teaspoon freshly ground black pepper

1 teaspoon fresh rosemary, chopped

1 teaspoon fresh mint, chopped

3 cloves garlic, minced

1. Put the olive oil in your hands and rub the oil all over the lamb.

2. Put the lamb in the slow cooker and sprinkle it all over with the salt, pepper, rosemary, mint, and garlic, rubbing the spices onto the meat.

3. Cover and cook on Low for 6 to 8 hours. Do not cook on High.

4. Season with additional salt and pepper if desired.

Serve the lamb with a lively sugar-free mint sauce. Make it by chopping together ½ cup fresh mint leaves and ½ cup fresh parsley leaves. Stir in about ½ cup olive oil, salt and pepper to taste, and a squeeze or so of fresh lemon juice. If you feel it needs some sweetening, stir in a teaspoon of honey.

Pork Vindaloo

It's all about spicy for me, and this recipe hits the spot. Vary this for yourself by tempering the chili peppers.

Makes 4 to 6 servings.

2 tablespoons olive oil

4 onions, sliced thin

6 chilies, such as jalapenos, habaneros, or a combination, seeded and sliced (wear gloves to do this)

1 teaspoon turmeric

1 teaspoon ground coriander

1½ teaspoons garam masala

½ teaspoon cinnamon

2½ lbs pork butt, trimmed and cut into cubes

2 tablespoons apple cider vinegar

2 tablespoons fresh ginger, grated

10 cloves garlic, peeled

1 teaspoon dry mustard powder

14.5-oz can diced tomatoes, undrained

1. Heat oil in a skillet over medium-high heat and add slices of 2 onions. Cook, stirring frequently, for about 3 minutes, until onions are translucent.

2. Add chilies, turmeric, coriander, garam masala, and cinnamon, stirring constantly to coat the onions and chilies with the spices. Remove from heat.

3. Put pork chunks into the slow cooker, and add the onion spice mix. Add the garlic cloves, cider vinegar, ginger, dry mustard, and tomatoes, and stir well. Place the slices from the remaining 2 onions over the pork mixture. Cover and cook on Low for 6 to 8 hours or on High for 4 to 5 hours.

> The whole cloves of garlic in this recipe are a treat to eat. The garlic gets soft and loses its bite and is instead infused with the other spices.

Wine-Not Beef Stew

Okay, so this is a stew cooked in lots of red wine. But it's delicious—and it's a great way to use up leftover red wine from a party or picnic.

Makes 6 to 8 servings.

4 tablespoons olive oil

2 cloves garlic, minced

4 lbs beef stew meat

1 onion, sliced thin

½ cup fresh mushrooms, sliced

1 teaspoon dried rosemary

Salt and pepper to taste

3 cups dry red wine

1. Heat the oil in a skillet and add the garlic. Brown the stew pieces in the oil until lightly browned on all sides. Transfer to the slow cooker.

2. Add the onion to the skillet and cook, stirring, until onions are translucent, about 3 minutes. Add the mushrooms and stir, cooking, another minute or so. Remove from heat and add the rosemary. Season the mushroom/onion mix with salt and freshly ground pepper. Add to the slow cooker.

3. Pour the wine over everything in the slow cooker. Cover and cook on Low for 8 to 10 hours or on High for 6 to 7 hours.

> Wine adds not only moisture but flavor. Wines can be a great substitute for a fattier ingredient, like excess butter or oil, and they have their own flavor profiles, so you can experiment with using a fruitier wine or a more acidic, tannin-rich wine. (Don't use sweet wines in savory dishes, however.)

Spinach-Stuffed Tenderloin

This super-easy meal tastes like you went to a lot of trouble. So do it for family, friends, or yourself, and spend the time you didn't need to spend on preparation or cooking on enjoying the rest of your day.

Makes 4 servings.

2 teaspoons olive oil

⅓ cup onion, diced

2 cloves garlic, minced

10-ounce package frozen chopped spinach, thawed and squeezed dry

¼ cup soft, fresh goat's milk cheese (chevre) or feta cheese, finely crumbled

1 teaspoon grated lemon zest

Salt and pepper to taste

1 lb pork tenderloin

Meat thermometer

1. In a skillet over medium-high heat, cook the onions in the olive oil until translucent, about 3 minutes. Add the garlic and continue to cook for a minute or so. Remove from heat and allow to cool slightly. Stir in the spinach and cheese. Sprinkle with lemon zest and season with salt and pepper.

2. Put the tenderloin on a cutting board, and using a large, sharp knife, cut lengthwise through the center, making sure you don't cut it in half. Lay the piece of meat open and flat on the cutting board. Place plastic wrap over it, and pound it with a meat mallet until it is about ½-inch thick. Remove and discard the plastic.

3. Scoop the spinach filling onto the meat and spread it out evenly, leaving room at the ends. Roll it up like a jellyroll. Secure with kitchen twine or just lay the meat seam side down in the slow cooker. Once in the slow cooker, cover and cook on Low for 4 to 5 hours, or on High for about 2 hours, until the meat registers about 145 degrees on a meat thermometer.

Variations:

You can play with the stuffing for this recipe in all sorts of ways.

* Chop up some mushrooms and cook them with the onions and garlic.
* Skip the cheese.
* Toast some almonds or pine nuts and add them to the spinach.
* Try a pinch of nutmeg.

Chapter 5

Chicken and Turkey Dishes

*G*reat news, low-carb eaters: There are many, many ways to prepare poultry dishes in the slow cooker. With a supply of ingredients stocked in your low-carb pantry and fridge—including lots of herbs and spices—you will learn that it's easy to prepare healthy and filling meals featuring your favorite cuts of chicken and turkey. There are plenty of ideas for varying the ingredients in the dishes, as well, so get creative and experiment with flavors and textures.

Simply Sensational Roast Chicken

The slow cooking yields tender, fragrant meat. If you want crisp skin, put the cooked chicken under the broiler in the oven for about 5 minutes. But, chances are, it won't matter to you when this is done.

1 onion, cut into thick slivers

1 carrot, sliced

4- to 5-lb whole chicken

1 lemon

1 teaspoon dried thyme

1 teaspoon dried sage

1 teaspoon sea salt

1 teaspoon ground black pepper

Fresh rosemary for garnish, if desired

1. Place the slivers of onion and the sliced carrot in the slow cooker. Put the chicken on top of the vegetables. Squeeze the lemon over everything, then slice it into rounds and put a couple of the slices in the cavity of the bird. Season all over with thyme, sage, salt, and pepper.

2. Cover and cook on Low for 6 to 8 hours or on High for 3 to 4 hours. Season with additional salt and pepper, and garnish with fresh rosemary, if desired.

You could substitute an already-made blend of spices called Poultry Seasoning for the thyme and sage. The poultry blend contains those herbs, as well as marjoram, parsley, and sometimes savory and rosemary.

Turkey Mole

This dark and thick sauce is made with a combination of spices, unsweetened cocoa powder, and butter. It has a depth of flavor that's incredible and is wonderful accompanied by a big, green salad.

Makes 4 to 6 servings.

1½-lb boneless, skinless turkey breast

2 tablespoons olive oil

1 onion, diced

3 cloves garlic, minced

2 tablespoons chili powder

2 tablespoons unsweetened cocoa powder

2 teaspoons ground cumin

1 teaspoon ground coriander

¼ teaspoon ground cinnamon

14.5-oz can diced tomatoes, drained

1½ cups chicken stock or broth

3 tablespoons unsalted butter

1 chipotle chili in adobo sauce, finely chopped

2 teaspoons adobo sauce

1 tablespoon arrowroot

Salt and pepper to taste

1. Rinse turkey and pat dry with paper towels. Trim fat, and cut turkey into 1-inch cubes.

2. Heat oil in a skillet over medium-high heat. Add onions and garlic, and cook, stirring frequently, for 3 minutes, or until onions are translucent. Reduce the heat to low, and stir in chili powder, cocoa powder, cumin, coriander, and cinnamon. Cook for 1 minute, stirring constantly. Scrape mixture into the slow cooker.

3. Add turkey, tomatoes, stock, butter, chipotle chili, and adobo sauce to the cooker, and stir well. Cook on Low for 4 to 6 hours or on High for 2 to 3 hours, or until turkey is cooked through and no longer pink.

4. If cooking on Low, raise the heat to High. Mix arrowroot with 2 tablespoons cold water in a small cup. Stir mixture into the slow cooker, and cook for an additional 10 to 20 minutes, or until the liquid is bubbling and has slightly thickened. Season to taste with salt and pepper.

Mole is a thick and rich sauce made with unsweetened chocolate that dates back to the Aztec empire in Mexico. Legend states that King Montezuma, thinking that Cortez was a god, served mole at a banquet to receive him. The word mole comes from the Nahuatl word "milli," which means sauce or "concoction."

Indonesian Chicken Curry

This form of curry became very popular in the Netherlands in the nineteenth century because they had substantial land holdings in the part of Southeast Asia that is now Indonesia. It is a fairly mild curry, and the coconut milk makes it appear creamy.

Makes 4 to 6 servings.

1½ lbs boneless, skinless chicken breasts

1 tablespoon Asian sesame oil

2 tablespoons grated fresh ginger

3 scallions, white parts and 4 inches of green tops, chopped

3 cloves garlic, minced

2 tablespoons curry powder

1 teaspoon ground cumin

½ red bell pepper, seeds and ribs removed, cut into 1-inch squares

1 cup chicken broth or stock

1 cup coconut milk

2 tablespoons rice wine vinegar

1 tablespoon raw honey

1 cup bok choy, sliced

2 ripe plum tomatoes, cored, seeded, and cut into sixths

1 tablespoon arrowroot

Salt and pepper to taste

1. Rinse chicken and pat dry with paper towels. Cut chicken into 1-inch cubes.

2. Heat oil in a skillet over medium-high heat. Add ginger, scallions, and garlic, and cook, stirring frequently, for 30 seconds, or until fragrant. Reduce the heat to low, and stir in curry powder and cumin. Cook for 1 minute, stirring constantly. Scrape mixture into slow cooker.

3. Add chicken, red bell pepper, stock, coconut milk, vinegar, and honey to the slow cooker, and stir well. Cook on Low for 3 to 5 hours or on High for about 2 hours, or until chicken is cooked through. Add bok choy and tomatoes, and cook for 1 more hour on Low or 30 minutes on High, or until bok choy is crisp-tender.

4. If cooking on Low, raise the heat to High. Mix arrowroot with 2 tablespoons cold water in a small cup. Stir mixture into the slow cooker, and cook for an additional 15 to 20 minutes, or until the liquid is bubbling and has slightly thickened. Season to taste with salt and pepper.

Frequently, coconut milk separates in the can with the liquid on the bottom and a thick layer of coconut on the top. Whisk it briskly until the lumps are gone because they will not break up well with the low heat in the slow cooker.

Cornish Hens with Fresh Greens

Cornish hens are as easy to make as dishes with chicken pieces, but there's something about them that makes the meal seem extra-special.

Makes 4 to 6 servings.

2 tablespoons olive oil

1 small onion, minced

1 garlic clove, minced

2 small Cornish game hens, split in two, skin removed

1 head Swiss chard, washed, coarse stems removed, and leaves chopped in large pieces

1 head Escarole, washed, trimmed, and chopped in large pieces

½ cup chicken stock or broth

1 lb baby spinach leaves

Salt and pepper to taste

1. Heat oil in a small skillet over medium-high heat, and cook onions and garlic about 3 minutes, or until onion is translucent. Scrape mixture into slow cooker.

2. Place Cornish hens on top of onion mixture, and top with Swiss chard, escarole, and stock.

3. Cover the slow cooker and cook on Low for 6 to 7 hours or on High for 3 to 4 hours, or until chicken is tender and cooked through.

4. Add the baby spinach and cook for another 20 to 30 minutes. Season with salt and pepper.

> The Cornish game hen is a young, immature chicken, which is technically not supposed to be over 5 weeks of age or more than 2 pounds. It's the result of crossing the Cornish game and Plymouth or White Rock chicken breeds.

Chicken Thighs Provençale

Skinless chicken thighs are a great cut to use for this recipe, as they tend to release a lot of juices during slow cooking because they are fattier that the breast. The juices help baste the pieces, resulting in meat that falls from the bones.

Makes 4 to 6 servings.

6 to 8 chicken thighs, skins removed
1 tablespoon herbes de Provence
½ teaspoon salt
1 teaspoon freshly ground black pepper
Juice of 1 lemon

1. Place the thighs in the slow cooker. Sprinkle with the herbs, salt, and pepper. Squeeze the lemon over the meat.

2. Cover and cook on low for 8 to 10 hours, or on High for about 6 hours. Serve the chicken hot—or allow it to cool, remove it from the bones, and shred it over a salad of fresh greens.

This delightfully easy-to-prepare dish is fragrant with rosemary, thyme, marjoram, and more.

Chicken and Asparagus

This is an interesting dish since, along with the asparagus it includes Bibb lettuce, an odd combination that turns to magic in the slow cooker.

Makes 4 to 6 servings.

6 chicken thighs, skin removed

2 cups chicken stock or broth

3 tablespoons fresh parsley, chopped

1 tablespoon fresh thyme

1 tablespoon fresh rosemary, chopped

1 tablespoon fresh tarragon

1 bay leaf

2 cloves garlic, minced

8 stalks asparagus, tough bottoms removed, cut into ½-inch pieces

2 heads Bibb lettuce, trimmed and cut into quarters

Salt and pepper to taste

1. Rinse chicken and pat dry with paper towels. Preheat the oven broiler, and line a broiler pan with heavy-duty aluminum foil. Broil chicken pieces for 3 minutes per side, or until browned.

2. Add stock, parsley, thyme, rosemary, tarragon, bay leaf, garlic, and asparagus pieces to the cooker, and stir well. Arrange chicken pieces in the slow cooker, and cook on Low for 5 to 7 hours or on High for 2 to 3 hours, or until chicken is almost cooked through.

3. If cooking on Low, raise the heat to High. Add lettuce, and cook for another 30 minutes, or until lettuce is wilted, chicken is tender, and mixture is bubbling. Remove and discard bay leaf, and season to taste with salt and pepper.

> Other spring vegetables you could add include a handful or so of young dandelion leaves or ramps (add with the lettuce).

Everyday Turkey Breast

You might find yourself preparing this at the end of every week so you can slice into it as your week gets busy. It makes a lovely, finished meat that can be used to top salads, roll in lettuce leaves, or even eat out of the fridge.

Makes 4 to 6 servings.

4-lb boneless, skinless turkey breast
½ teaspoon salt
¼ teaspoon pepper
1 tablespoon fresh rosemary, chopped
1 tablespoon fresh parsley, chopped
½ cup chicken stock or broth

1. Place the turkey in the slow cooker. Sprinkle with salt and pepper, add herbs, and add stock.

2. Cover and cook on Low for 7 to 9 hours or on High for 4 to 6 hours, or until the meat is cooked through.

Variation:
For easy-to-make, healthy, and delicious snacks, put cut cooked turkey onto a Romaine lettuce leaf, and top with avocado slices, tomato slices, slivered almonds, and diced red onion. Roll the filling up in the leaf and enjoy.

Chicken and Mushrooms

Adding sherry to the mushrooms while sautéing them will fill your kitchen with the delightful aromas of hazelnut and caramel. Imagine what the meal tastes like when it's finished!

Makes 4 servings.

4 boneless chicken breasts

3 tablespoons olive oil

1 onion, sliced thin

2 cloves garlic, minced

2 lbs fresh mushrooms, stems removed and chopped

1 teaspoon sage

¼ cup dry sherry

10-oz package frozen spinach, thawed and squeezed to remove excess moisture

Salt and pepper to taste

Heavy cream if desired

Fresh parsley for garnish

1. Place the chicken breasts between sheets of waxed paper and pound them with a meat mallet until they are about ½ inch thick.

2. In a large skillet, heat the olive oil over medium-high heat. Add the onion and garlic and cook, stirring, until the onion is translucent, about 3 minutes. Add the mushrooms and continue to cook, stirring constantly, until they begin to soften, another 3 minutes. Remove from heat. Add the sage and sherry and stir to combine.

3. Put the chicken breasts in the slow cooker, and distribute the spinach over the meat. Scoop the mushroom mixture over the meat and spinach. Sprinkle with some salt and freshly ground pepper. Cover and cook on Low for 8 to 10 hours or on High for about 6 hours.

4. Before serving, stir in heavy cream, if desired, not more than ½ cup. Garnish with sprigs of fresh parsley.

Sherry hails from Spain originally and is a fortified wine made with white wine grapes. Dry sherry has no added sugar, which makes it suitable for use in a low-carb diet. There are just 6 carbs in ½ cup.

Turkey Kabobs

This is fun food for the kids—and the adults! Vary the vegetables you use depending on what's super-fresh.

Makes 4 to 6 servings.

⅓ cup olive oil

1 tablespoon herbes de Provence

2 cloves garlic, mashed

¼ teaspoon salt

½ teaspoon pepper

4-lb boneless, skinless breast turkey, cut into cubes

1 red bell pepper, seeded and cut into large chunks

1 green bell pepper, seeded and cut into large chunks

1 onion, cut into thick wedges

1 zucchini, cut into thin slices

2 quarts ripe cherry tomatoes

Wooden skewers, cut or broken into sizes to fit into the slow cooker

1. In a large bowl, combine the olive oil, herbes, garlic, salt, and pepper, and stir to combine. Add the turkey, peppers, onions, and zucchini, and toss to coat all.

2. Put the turkey and vegetables onto the skewers, working in the cherry tomatoes. Put the skewers in the slow cooker as you finish them. Pour the remaining dressing over the skewers.

3. Cook on Low for 3 to 4 hours or on High for 2 to 3 hours until turkey is cooked through and vegetables are crisp-tender.

Spice it up by adding some cayenne to the dressing or by including slices of fresh seeded, sliced jalapenos or other hot peppers.

Poached Poultry Breasts

You can use chicken or turkey in this recipe. What I like to do is make this mid-week in the summer, then when guests come on the weekend, I have delicious and tender cooked chicken to use for multiple variations of chicken salad.

Makes 4 to 8 servings.

4 to 6 chicken boneless, skinless chicken breasts

1 tablespoon olive oil

1 onion, chopped fine

2 cloves garlic, minced

2 cups chicken broth

2 cups water

Juice of ½ lemon

1 bouquet garni (see sidebar)

1 teaspoon whole white peppercorns

1. Place chicken breasts in the slow cooker.

2. Heat oil in a skillet and add the onions and garlic. Cook until the onions are translucent, 3 to 5 minutes. Transfer the onion mixture to the slow cooker. Cover the breasts with the chicken broth and water, and squeeze the lemon juice over everything. Add the peppercorns and the bouquet garni.

3. Cover and cook on Low for 8 to 10 hours or on High for about 7 hours. Remove the bouquet garni after 4 hours. Remove the cooked chicken with a slotted spoon, and allow to cool thoroughly. Put in a bowl covered with plastic wrap, and serve cold—perfect for chicken salad.

The bouquet garni is a bundle of herbs traditionally used to flavor soups, stews, and sauces. While there's some variation, use the classic combination for this recipe. Take 2 sprigs of fresh thyme, 2 sprigs of parsley, and a large bay leaf. Tie the herbs together with kitchen string.

Turkey Meatballs on Top of Zucchini

Mix things up with this family-friendly meal.

Makes 4 to 6 servings.

1 lb ground turkey

1 egg

½ onion, minced

1 tablespoon fresh parsley, chopped fine

2 cloves garlic, put through a garlic press

Salt and pepper to taste

2 large zucchini, sliced thin

14.5-oz can diced tomatoes, undrained

1. In a large bowl, combine the turkey, egg, onion, parsley, garlic, and a sprinkling of salt and pepper. Stir thoroughly.

2. Put the zucchini slices in the slow cooker. Form the meat into meatballs, and put them on top of the zucchini. Add the tomatoes over everything.

3. Cover and cook on Low for 4 to 6 hours or on High for 3 to 4 hours, until meatballs are cooked through and zucchini is tender. Season with additional salt and pepper if desired.

Substitute any other kind of ground meat in this recipe. With the egg, onion, garlic, and parsley, you'll still fashion delicious meatballs. Vary the spices to create different flavor profiles.

Chicken Stuffed with Kale and Cheese

This is a low-carb and overall healthier variation on the French dish that took America by storm in the 1980s, chicken cordon bleu, which is a ham-and-cheese stuffed culet that's breaded and fried. It's hard to beat fried, salty, and creamy, but this slow-cooked recipe is a worthy adversary.

Makes 4 servings.

4 boneless, skinless chicken breasts

Salt and pepper for seasoning

¼ teaspoon dried oregano

½ teaspoon onion powder

½ teaspoon cayenne pepper

2 cups kale leaves, chopped

1 lb Swiss cheese, cut into thick strips

Kitchen twine

½ cup dry white wine

1. The breasts should be on the thin side so they roll up easily. If they're thicker than ½ to ¼ inch, put them between pieces of waxed paper and use a meat mallet to pound them thin.

2. Sprinkle salt, pepper, oregano, onion powder, and cayenne on both sides of the cutlets. Put a layer of chopped kale in the center of each breast, lay a strip or so of Swiss cheese over to cover it, and top with some additional kale. Wrap the rolls tightly and secure with kitchen twine.

3. Lay the rolls in the slow cooker. Add the wine. Cover and cook on Low for 6 to 8 hours, or on High for about 5 hours, or until the juices run clear and the cheese is melted. If you want to "crisp" the outside, transfer the rolls to a foil-lined baking sheet and put them under the broiler for a few minutes.

Variation:
To add decadence to this recipe, cook 4 strips of bacon in the microwave until crispy, and add one to each roll before wrapping and securing the filling inside.

Tandoori Chicken

I am a huge fan of the spices in this dish. While tandoori is typically done with a dry finish, this makes a succulent and juicy dish. Serve over cauliflower "rice" with a salad of fresh greens on the side.

Makes 4 to 6 servings.

1½ cups nonfat plain Greek yogurt

⅓ cup sour cream

Juice from ½ lemon

½ teaspoon ground ginger

1 teaspoon ground cumin

1 teaspoon ground coriander

½ teaspoon paprika (sweet)

1 teaspoon turmeric

1 teaspoon salt

½ teaspoon cayenne pepper

4 lbs chicken pieces, bones in, skin removed

1. In a bowl, combine the yogurt, sour cream, and lemon juice. In another small bowl, combine the ginger, cumin, coriander, paprika, turmeric, salt, and cayenne pepper. Whisk the spices to combine well. Add to the yogurt mix and stir to mix thoroughly.

2. Put the chicken pieces in a shallow baking dish and cover with the yogurt/spice mix. Cover the dish with plastic wrap and put it in the refrigerator. Allow to marinate overnight, or at least 8 hours.

3. Put the marinated chicken and the sauce in the slow cooker. Cover and cook on Low for 8 to 10 hours, or on High for 4 to 6 hours, until the chicken is cooked through.

There is a lively and ongoing debate about whether yogurt is acceptable on a low-carb diet. In the research I've done, 8 ounces of nonfat Greek yogurt has 8 grams of carbohydrates, so this dish calls for about 12 grams overall. But there are so many nutritional benefits of Greek yogurt, and in the end, the amount is being divided by 4 to 6 for serving in this recipe. It's so yummy. It's a great treat in many ways.

Super-Tender Chicken

This dish can be served as-is with various vegetable side dishes, or additional vegetables can be added to it to make a stew or thick soup. The almond flour is a low-carb substitute for wheat flour, and along with the coconut milk, gives the dish an interesting nutty flavor.

Makes 4 to 6 servings.

½ cup almond flour
Salt and pepper
8 chicken thighs, skin removed
2 tablespoons olive oil
1 onion, diced
1 cup dry white wine
1 cup chicken stock
1 teaspoon fresh tarragon
1 cup coconut milk
Salt and pepper to taste

1. Put almond flour, salt, and pepper in a shallow bowl and whisk to combine. Dip chicken thighs into flour, turning to coat, and shake off excess flour and set aside.

2. Heat oil in a large skillet, and add the chicken pieces. Brown the chicken on both sides, about 3 minutes a side. Transfer browned pieces to the slow cooker. Add the onion and, if necessary, some additional oil, and cook the onion for about 3 minutes, until translucent. Sprinkle a tablespoon or two of almond flour on the onions and stir to coat.

3. Add wine to the pan and stir, dislodging browned bits. Add chicken stock and bring continue to cook, stirring, while liquid thickens, about 10 minutes. Add tarragon, and pour liquid onto the chicken.

4. Cover and cook on Low for 5 to 6 hours or on High for 3 to 4 hours. Add the coconut milk and cook an additional 15 to 30 minutes until the liquid is bubbling. Season with additional salt and pepper.

> It's easy to make your own almond flour. Put ½ to ¾ cup unsalted whole almonds in a food processor and pulse until the nuts are completely broken down. This will yield about a cup of the flour.

Sunny Thyme Chicken

This recipe is so named because there's lots of lemon in it, too, and the combo of bright citrus, aromatic thyme, and—of course—hearty (and healthy) garlic, makes for a meal that harnesses the produce of the sun.

Makes 4 to 6 servings.

3 to 4 lbs chicken pieces, bones in, skins removed

1 head garlic

3 sprigs fresh thyme

2 lemons

½ cup chicken stock or broth

Salt and pepper to taste

1. Place the chicken pieces in the slow cooker.

2. Remove the peels from the garlic cloves, but don't cut them. Place the whole cloves of garlic in with the chicken.

3. Remove the leaves from the thyme stems. Place half the leaves over the chicken pieces. Cut the lemons in half and remove any seeds. Squeeze the juice over the chicken. Season with salt and pepper, and top with the chicken stock or broth.

4. Cover and cook on Low for 8 to 10 hours or on High for 4 to 5 hours. In the last half hour of cooking, add the remaining half of the thyme to the cooker, stir, and continue to cook.

The whole garlic cloves will poach in the broth as the chicken cooks. Poaching softens the flavor of the garlic so it's not as pungent and strong as when it's raw. Like roasted garlic, the poached cloves are delicious mashed. You can mash them in the sauce before serving, or you can strain them out of the dish, depending on your preference.

Barbecued Chicken Pieces

The slow cooker is truly the place to make the best barbecued chicken pieces. The long, low-heat cooking process cooks the meat to juicy perfection, and all you have to do to get that delicious crunchy barbecued skin is light the grill, brush the pieces with sauce, and grill them until they're just like you like them. So easy and so good!

4 lbs chicken pieces (drumsticks, thighs, and wings; not breasts)

1 lemon (or lime)

10-oz jar of your favorite barbecue sauce (no sugar added)

1. Trim the chicken pieces of any excess fat and skin. If you're including wings, cut them into "drumettes" and "flats." These are the two parts of the wing you want to use. Do this by extending the chicken wing. You'll see it has three parts: the tip, the middle (flat), and the end (drumette). Using a sharp knife, cut the wing at the two joints to separate the three parts. Discard the tips (or save to make chicken stock).

2. Pour some of the barbecue sauce into the slow cooker (enough to coat the bottom). Put the chicken pieces on top. Squeeze the juice from the lemon over the chicken pieces, being sure to remove the lemon seeds.

3. Pour a small amount of sauce over the pieces. You should have about half a jar of barbecue sauce remaining. Cover and cook on Low for 6 hours or on High for 4 hours.

4. Light a grill or preheat the broiler in your oven to high. When the grill is hot, remove the chicken pieces from the slow cooker with a slotted spoon and put them on a platter. Use a pastry brush to spread additional barbecue sauce on the individual pieces. Put the meat on the grill or on a foil-lined baking sheet under the broiler. Grill or broil for about 5 minutes a side—that's it—until the skin is crispy. Serve with whatever sauce is left.

It's pretty easy to find sugar-free barbecue sauce. Even if the label says it's sugar-free, double-check the ingredients. You want to be sure there are no artificial sweeteners added and that corn syrup is not an ingredient. If you want something really special, go online and research low-carb, sugar-free barbecue sauce. There are many great recipes.

Chicken and Clams

This is a "surf and turf" indulgence that'll have you coming back for more.

Makes 4 to 6 servings.

6 pieces of chicken, bone in and skinless

Salt and pepper

2 tablespoons olive oil

1 medium onion, diced

1 tablespoon Old Bay Seasoning

1 cup water

2 dozen littleneck clams, rinsed in several changes of water until water runs clear, and drained

½ cup fresh parsley, chopped

1. Season the chicken pieces with salt and pepper. Heat the oil over medium-high heat in a large skillet. Cook the chicken, turning every so often, until the chicken is browned on all sides.

2. Transfer the chicken to the slow cooker, then cook the onion in the oil for 3 to 5 minutes, until translucent. Remove from heat and stir in the Old Bay Seasonings. Add to the slow cooker with the chicken.

3. Add the water. Cover and cook on low for 5 to 6 hours. Turn the heat to High so that the liquid is bubbling.

4. Add the clams, replace the cover, and cook an additional 30 to 40 minutes, or until the clams are opened. Garnish with fresh parsley.

Old Bay Seasoning is commonly used on crabs, especially in the Chesapeake Bay area in Maryland. It's a blend of celery and spices, including paprika. And it has zero carbs!

Nutty Chicken Tenders

This dish combines heat from jalapenos with the creamy nuttiness of peanut butter. You'll want to eat the tenders right out of the slow cooker, using forks or long toothpicks to spear them and slather them in the sauce.

Makes 4 to 6 servings.

½ teaspoon ground cumin

½ teaspoon ground cinnamon

½ teaspoon salt

½ teaspoon freshly ground pepper

2 to 3 lbs boneless, skinless chicken, cut into 2-inch pieces

3 tablespoons olive oil

2 cups diced fresh tomatoes, seeds removed

2 generous tablespoons of all-natural peanut butter (all-natural peanut butters contain no sugar or additional salt)

1 tablespoon apple cider vinegar

3 cloves garlic, crushed

1 fresh jalapeno, sliced, all seeds removed

1. Mix cumin, cinnamon, salt, and pepper in a bowl. Add chicken pieces and stir to coat.

2. Heat olive oil in a skillet over medium high heat, and add the chicken pieces, stirring to brown them on all sides. Transfer the pieces to the slow cooker.

3. In a blender or food processor, combine the tomatoes, peanut butter, vinegar, garlic, and jalapeno, making a paste. Slather this over the chicken pieces. Cover and cook on Low for 4 to 6 hours, or on High for about 2 hours.

Variation:
Substitute bone-in, skinless chicken thighs for the boneless pieces. Reduce the slow cooker time by about an hour, and finish the cooking process on a hot grill. Serve the sauce on the side. Delicious!

Chicken and Artichokes

You'll delight at the low-carb goodness of this dish that features lots of flavors. The sauce is thickened at the end, making it almost like a stew.

Makes 4 to 6 servings.

2 lbs boneless, skinless chicken thighs

Salt and pepper

14.5-oz can diced tomatoes, with juice

14-oz jar artichoke hearts, drained

½ cup red onion, chopped

½ cup pitted kalamata olives, sliced

1 cup chicken broth or stock

1 tablespoon quick-cooking tapioca

1 tablespoon fresh Italian parsley, chopped

1 teaspoon dried thyme

½ teaspoon red pepper flakes

1. Put the chicken pieces in the slow cooker, and sprinkle with salt and pepper.

2. In a bowl, combine the tomatoes (with juice), artichoke hearts, onion, olives, chicken broth, tapioca, parsley, thyme, and red pepper flakes. Pour over chicken.

3. Cover and cook on Low for 5 to 6 hours, or on High for 3 to 4 hours, until chicken is tender and cooked through.

Variation:
This dish is also delicious made with tofu, another low-carb source of protein.

Chicken with Kale

The nice thing about kale in the slow cooker is that it is less tender than spinach, so it retains its body and color better. Kale is one of the healthiest of leafy greens, so eat up.

Makes 4 to 6 servings.

2 to 3 lbs chicken thighs, skin removed

2 tablespoons olive oil

½ small onion, minced

4 cloves garlic, minced

1 teaspoon red pepper flakes

2 lbs kale, washed and dried

½ cup chicken stock or broth

Salt and pepper to taste

1. Put the chicken pieces in the slow cooker.

2. Heat the oil in a skillet over medium-high heat, and cook the onions and garlic, stirring, for about 3 minutes. Add the red pepper flakes. Stir in and remove from heat. Scrape from the pan over the chicken pieces.

3. Top the chicken with the kale, tearing the leaves into smaller pieces if desired. Add the chicken stock. Cover and cook on Low for 8 to 10 hours or on High for about 6 hours, until the chicken is cooked through. Season with salt and pepper before serving.

Variation:

Here's an easy way to dress this dish up if you're inspired. Use a slotted spoon to remove the cooked chicken breasts. Keep them warm on a plate. Then scoop out the cooked kale into a bowl and cover to keep warm. Starting with just a sprinkle, add some xanthan gum to the warm sauce. Use a whisk to incorporate it as quickly and evenly as possible. Add more xanthan as necessary to thicken the sauce to a desired consistency. Just remember that a little goes a long way.

Asian Chicken in Napa Cabbage

Who needs the carbs in burritos when you can fill Napa cabbage leaves with delectable fillings like this Asian-spiced chicken? The great thing is that the chicken can cook all day, and when you get home all you need to do is steam the leaves, fill, roll, and eat!

Makes 6 to 8 servings.

2 lbs boneless chicken breast tenders

8-oz can water chestnuts, drained

1 cup white mushrooms, stems removed

4 scallions

3 cloves garlic, crushed

3 tablespoons tamari

1 tablespoon raw honey

1 teaspoon white wine vinegar

3 tablespoons olive oil

Guar or xanthan

8 outer leaves from a large Napa cabbage

½ cup almond slices, toasted (optional)

1. Cut the chicken pieces into thin strips, and place in the slow cooker.

2. Place the water chestnuts, mushroom caps, scallions, and garlic in a food processor or blender and pulse until they are the consistency of salsa, with some chunks. Scrape over chicken.

3. In a small bowl, combine tamari, honey, vinegar, and oil. Whisk to combine well, and pour over chicken and other ingredients. Cover and cook on Low for 4 to 6 hours or on High for about 3 hours, until chicken is cooked through.

4. When ready, trim the tough ends of the cabbage leaves. Heat about a half inch of water in a large skillet and poach the leaves in the boiling water until just soft. Place on a paper towel to absorb excess moisture.

5. When cool enough, spoon chicken mixture onto a leaf. Top with some toasted almonds if desired.

Tamari is soy sauce. The difference between it and the more commercially available brands on the market are that tamari is made with just soybeans, whereas the others contain wheat. The flavor is deeper and richer.

Chicken Parmesan

This low-carb variation doesn't have the breading normally used with chicken Parmesan. But with the sauce and cheese, it's every bit as good.

Makes 4 servings.

4 boneless, skinless chicken breasts

Garlic powder

Salt and pepper

Italian seasoning mix

Parmesan cheese, grated

1 cup no-sugar spaghetti sauce (Prego and Classico are among the popular brands that make these)

8 ounces shredded mozzarella cheese

1. Place the chicken breasts in the slow cooker. Season by sprinkling over them the garlic powder, salt, pepper, Italian seasoning, and a generous shaking of Parmesan cheese. Pour the spaghetti sauce over the meat.

2. Cover and cook on Low for 6 hours or on High for 4 hours.

3. Uncover and top the chicken with the mozzarella cheese. Cover and continue to cook on Low for another hour or on High for another 30 minutes.

Rather than sprinkle the meat with the seasonings, you can add them to your spaghetti sauce before pouring it on the chicken. You can also try a marinara sauce that has basil or red peppers, so long as there is no sugar added.

Chicken Cacciatore

Cacciatore is Italian for "hunter's style," and since Italians in all regions are hunters, this dish is almost a national one. Though several meats can be featured in a cacciatore, they all include tomatoes, onions, pancetta, and mushrooms.

Makes 4 to 6 servings.

6 chicken pieces, skin removed

¼ cup olive oil

2 large onions, halved and thinly sliced

2 cloves garlic, minced

1 lb cremini mushrooms, wiped with a damp paper towel, trimmed, and sliced

28-oz can diced tomatoes, undrained

½ cup dry white wine

1 tablespoon fresh thyme

1 tablespoon fresh sage, chopped

1 tablespoon fresh rosemary, chopped

Salt and pepper to taste

1. Rinse chicken and pat dry with paper towels. Preheat the oven broiler, and line a broiler pan with heavy-duty aluminum foil. Broil chicken pieces for 3 minutes per side, or until browned. Transfer pieces to the slow cooker.

2. Heat oil in a large skillet over medium-high heat. Add onions, garlic, and mushrooms and cook, stirring frequently, for 5 minutes, or until mushrooms begin to soften. Scrape mixture into the slow cooker.

3. Add tomatoes, wine, thyme, sage, and rosemary to the cooker, and stir well. Cook on Low for 6 to 8 hours or on High for 3 to 4 hours, or until chicken is cooked through, tender, and no longer pink. Season to taste with salt and pepper.

Most of the mushrooms we find in supermarkets are the same species, Agaricus bisporus. What makes the difference is their age. White button mushrooms are the youngest, cremini are in the middle, and Portobello is what we call them when they're big and old.

Chapter 6

Delicious Fishes and Seafood

*I*f you're a fan of seafood—and I definitely am—you have no worries about adding variety to your low-carb diet. Most fish is carb free, and there's nothing easier than popping some filets into the slow cooker with some lemon juice, butter, and white wine and coming home to dinner. You'll find there are many other ways to prepare low-carb, delicious recipes featuring a variety of fish, from crab-stuffed salmon filets to herbed trout to monkfish kabobs. Dig in!

Asian-Basted Salmon

The key to flavor in this recipe is to use fresh ginger. It dazzles the nose and the palette.

Makes 4 servings.

4 large salmon steaks (3 to 4 lbs total)

½ cup tamari

½ cup orange juice

4 tablespoon fresh ginger (peeled and minced)

3 cloves garlic, chopped

2 teaspoon toasted sesame oil

½ teaspoon chili sauce (Sriracha)

Xanthan (thickener)

Fresh parsley or cilantro for garnish, if desired

1. Spray the slow cooker with non-stick spray and put the fish in it.

2. In a bowl, combine the tamari, orange juice, ginger, garlic, sesame oil, and chili sauce. Pour over salmon steaks. Cover and cook on Low for 4 hours or on High for 1½ hours until fish is cooked through.

3. Transfer salmon steaks to a plate and cover to keep warm.

4. Sprinkle just a little xanthan onto sauce and whisk briskly to combine. Add a very small amount at a time until sauce is desired thickness. Serve over steaks and garnish with fresh parsley or cilantro.

While fresh oranges are not an acceptable fruit for a low-carb diet, orange juice doesn't have too many more grams of carbohydrates than lemon juice. This recipe calls for a small quantity, so no worries.

Tilapia Aioli

Tilapia is a mild, white meat fish, which is the kind you want for this recipe. The aioli is a homemade garlicky mayonnaise-type sauce that makes a dish that melts in your mouth.

Makes 2 to 4 servings.

1 lb tilapia filets

2 cloves garlic

1 egg

¼ teaspoon salt

2 tablespoons lemon juice

½ cup olive oil

2 tablespoons Parmesan cheese

¼ cup fresh parsley, chopped

1. Put tilapia filets in the slow cooker.

2. Make the aioli. In a blender or food processor, put the garlic, egg, salt, and lemon juice. Blend on high for about 30 seconds until well combined. With the blender running on low, pour the olive oil in slowly. The sauce will emulsify as you pour in the oil. Don't rush the process. When you've poured in all the oil and you have a thick sauce, turn off the blender. Pour the aioli over the fish. Sprinkle with Parmesan cheese.

3. Cover and cook on Low for about 2 to 3 hours, until the filets are cooked through. Garnish with fresh parsley.

Tilapia is one of many varieties of fish in the cichlid family. They mainly inhabit freshwater ponds, streams, and lakes and have been plentiful throughout time, with images of their capture in Egyptian hieroglyphics. Today the bulk of the tilapia in our stores comes from farm-raised fish, which is what keeps the price down.

Herbed Trout

For my family, trout is a fish that can satisfy both those who like a "fishier" fish (more dark meat) and those who like a milder fish (whiter meat). For me, it's a delicate-fleshed fish that still has lots of flavor.

Makes 2 to 4 servings.

2 brook trout, whole or fileted

1 lemon

Salt and pepper

1 teaspoon Italian seasoning

2 tablespoons unsalted butter

½ cup white wine

Fresh parsley for garnish

1. Line the slow cooker with aluminum foil, bringing it up over the sides so the cover goes on securely.

2. Put the whole trout or the filets in the slow cooker. Cut the lemon in half and squeeze the juice from each half over the fish, picking out any seeds. Season with salt and pepper, and sprinkle with Italian seasonings. Divide the 2 tablespoons of butter into 4 smaller tabs, and put on the filets. Pour the white wine over the fish.

3. Cover and cook on Low for 4 to 5 hours, until the filets are cooked through. Carefully lift out the foil and put the fish and sauce—on the foil—in a baking dish. It will be easier to use a spatula to lift off the filets or whole fish from the shallow-sided baking dish than from the slow cooker.

4. If you made filets, they're ready to serve. If you prepared the trout whole, see the sidebar on this page for directions to remove the bones.

If you prepared the trout whole, you will need to filet them. First, remove the fins along the side. Then make a gentle incision along the spine, sliding the top of the fish off (which should slide off fairly easily since it's cooked through). Grasp the tail to lift out the skeleton, including the head. This removes all the bones at once.

Crab-Stuffed Salmon Filets

Decadent and delicious, you'll feel like you're eating at a 5-star restaurant when you put these on your table.

Makes 4 to 6 servings.

8 oz cooked crabmeat (fresh is best, but imitation will work), flaked

¼ cup celery, minced

2 cloves garlic, minced

¼ cup red pepper, minced

1 teaspoon fresh parsley, chopped fine

¼ teaspoon salt

½ teaspoon freshly ground pepper

1 teaspoon fresh lemon juice

1 egg

¼ cup unsalted butter, melted

6 salmon filets (about 6 oz each)

1. Make the crabmeat stuffing by combining the crabmeat, celery, garlic, red pepper, parsley, salt, pepper, lemon juice, egg, and melted butter in a bowl. Stir well to combine and make a nice stuffing mix.

2. Make a slit in the side of the salmon filets and evenly divide the stuffing into the filets. Gently transfer each stuffed filet to the slow cooker.

3. Cover and cook on Low for 4 to 5 hours until fish is cooked through.

An excellent accompaniment to the stuffed salmon filets is spinach. Steam baby spinach leaves and make a pile of them in the center of a dinner plate. Place the stuffed salmon on top. Serve with lemon on the side. I'd splurge with a (small) glass of white wine!

Shrimp Scampi

Make these as an appetizer for a party. They're the perfect bite-sized food to spear with a fork or toothpick.

Makes 6 to 8 servings.

2 lbs medium-sized raw shrimp, shells removed

2 tablespoons olive oil

4 cloves garlic, minced

1 tablespoon red pepper flakes

14.5-oz can chopped tomatoes, with juice

1 teaspoon oregano

Salt and pepper to taste

1. Heat the oil in a skillet and add the garlic, stirring until it sizzles. Add the tomatoes, red pepper flakes, oregano, salt, and pepper. Stir to combine and cook for about 3 minutes.

2. Transfer sauce to the slow cooker. Place the shrimp on the sauce. Cover and cook on Low for 4 hours or on High for about 2 hours, until the shrimp are cooked through.

3. Serve straight out of the slow cooker with long forks or toothpicks.

Make a meal out of this dish by serving the shrimp with the sauce over spaghetti squash. Not only will it be very tasty, the colors will be very nice.

Tuna and Artichokes

Making this with fresh tuna steaks is the key to getting the best flavor. The chunks will flake nicely into the sauce when cooked through.

Makes 4 to 6 servings.

2 fresh tuna steaks, skins removed and cut into cubes

Salt and pepper

14.5-oz can diced tomatoes, with juice

14-oz jar artichoke hearts, drained

½ cup red onion, chopped

½ cup pitted kalamata olives, sliced

1 cup white wine

1 tablespoon quick-cooking tapioca

1 tablespoon fresh Italian parsley, chopped

½ teaspoon red pepper flakes

1. Put the tuna pieces in the slow cooker, and sprinkle with salt and pepper.

2. In a bowl, combine the tomatoes (with juice), artichoke hearts, onions, olives, wine, tapioca, parsley, and red pepper flakes. Pour over tuna.

3. Cover and cook on Low for 4 to 5 hours, or on High for 2 to 3 hours, until tuna is cooked through.

> The tapioca will thicken the sauce as it cooks, making an almost stew-like dish that's fragrant and hearty.

Tomato-Braised Tuna

Tuna is caught in the waters off Sicily, and in this recipe the gentle heat of the slow cooker glorifies this meaty fish while keeping it fairly rare. If you have any left over, you can add it to a mixed salad.

Makes 4 to 6 servings.

1 (1½ to 2-lb) tuna fillet in one thick slice
¼ cup olive oil, divided
½ small red onion, chopped
3 cloves garlic, minced
15.5-oz can diced tomatoes
1 teaspoon fresh basil, chopped
¼ teaspoon dried oregano
½ teaspoon dried rosemary
3 tablespoon capers, drained and rinsed
2 tablespoons fresh parsley, chopped
1 bay leaf
Salt and pepper to taste

1. Soak tuna in cold water for 10 minutes. Pat dry with paper towels.

2. Heat 2 tablespoons of the oil in a large skillet over medium-high heat. Add onion and garlic and cook, stirring frequently, for 3 minutes, or until onion is translucent. Scrape mixture into the slow cooker. Add diced tomatoes, herbs, capers, parsley, and bay leaf to the slow cooker and stir well. Cook on Low for 2 to 3 hours or on High for about 1 hour.

3. Heat remaining oil in the skillet over medium-high heat. Add tuna, and brown well on both sides. Add tuna to the slow cooker, and cook on Low for an additional 2 hours or on High for an additional hour or 90 minutes. Tuna should be cooked but still rare in the center. Remove and discard bay leaf, season to taste with salt and pepper, and serve hot.

Soaking the tuna in water removes a lot of its remaining blood, so that the finished dish is lighter in color and not bright red. The same treatment can be used on other dark fish, such as mackerel or bluefish.

Fish with Tomatoes and Fennel

In this colorful dish, fish fillets are cooked on top of a delicious an aromatic bed of vegetables scented with orange. Close your eyes and imagine you're dining on the Italian coast.

Makes 4 to 6 servings.

2 medium fennel bulbs

¼ cup olive oil

1 large onion, thinly sliced

2 cloves garlic, minced

28-oz can diced tomatoes, drained

1 tablespoon grated orange zest

1 tablespoon fennel seeds, crushed

2 lbs thick, firm-fleshed fish fillets (such as cod, halibut, or tilapia), cut into serving-sized pieces

Salt and pepper to taste

1. Discard stalks from fennel, and save for another use. Rinse fennel, cut in half lengthwise, and discard core and top layer of flesh. Slice fennel thinly and set aside.

2. Heat oil in a large skillet over medium-high heat. Add onion and garlic, and cook, stirring frequently, for 3 minutes, or until onion is translucent. Add fennel and cook for an additional 2 minutes. Scrape mixture into the slow cooker.

3. Add tomatoes, zest, orange juice, and fennel seeds to the slow cooker. Stir well to combine. Cook on Low for 5 to 7 hours, or on High for 2 to 3 hours, or until fennel is crisp-tender.

4. If cooking on Low, raise the heat to High. Season fish with salt and pepper, and place it on top of vegetables. Cover and cook for 30 to 45 minutes, or until fish is cooked through and flakes easily. Season to taste with salt and pepper.

The vegetable mixture can be cooked up to 2 days in advance and refrigerated, tightly covered. Reheat it in a microwave oven or over low heat, and return it to the slow cooker. Increase the heat to High and cook the fish just prior to serving, as described above.

Lemon-Tarragon Bluefish

Bluefish is one that people either love or hate. It's considered an oily fish, and it has an almost gamey taste. It's found all around the world, so it's a fish that has sustained us for millennia.

Makes 4 to 6 servings.

3 lbs bluefish fillet

2 tablespoons fresh tarragon, chopped

2 lemons

1 large onion, thinly sliced

Salt and pepper to taste

1. Make sure the fillets are free of bones. Put them skin side down into the slow cooker.

2. Sprinkle the tarragon over the fish, then squeeze the lemons over them. Remove any seeds. Thinly slice one of the squeezed lemons, and place the slices on the fish. Finally, top with the onion slices.

3. Cook on Low for 3 to 4 hours or on High for 1 to 2 hours, until fish is cooked through and flakes easily.

Variation:

✻ This simply prepared fish is also delicious chilled and served in lettuce wraps. Garnish with chopped cucumbers, cherry tomatoes, and a thin slice of avocado.

Monkfish with Cabbage, Pancetta, and Rosemary

Monkfish, sometimes called "poor man's lobster" because its sweet flavor and texture are similar to the prized crustacean, is popular in the regions bordering the Adriatic Sea in Italy.

Makes 4 to 6 servings.

½ small (1½ lbs) head Savoy or green cabbage

¼ lb pancetta, diced

2 lbs monkfish fillets, trimmed and cut into serving pieces

2 cloves garlic, minced

1 cup fish stock or broth

2 tablespoons fresh rosemary, chopped, or 2 teaspoon dried

1 tablespoon fresh parsley, chopped

2 teaspoon grated lemon zest

Salt and pepper to taste

1 tablespoon fresh parsley, chopped

1. Rinse and core cabbage. Cut into wedges and then shred cabbage. Bring a large pot of salted water to a boil. Add cabbage and boil for 4 minutes. Drain cabbage and place it in the slow cooker.

2. Cook pancetta in a heavy skillet over medium heat for 5 to 7 minutes, or until crisp. Remove pancetta from the skillet with a slotted spoon, and place it in the slow cooker. Raise the heat to high, and sear the monkfish in the fat on all sides, turning the pieces gently with tongs, until browned. Refrigerate fish.

3. Add garlic, stock, rosemary, parsley, and lemon zest to the slow cooker, and stir well. Cook on Low for 3 to 4 hours or on High for 1 to 2 hours, or until cabbage is almost tender.

4. If cooking on Low, raise the heat to High. Season monkfish with salt and pepper, and place it on top of the vegetables. Cook monkfish for 30 to 45 minutes, or until it is cooked through. Remove monkfish from the slow cooker, and keep it warm. Season the cabbage with salt and pepper.

5. To serve, mound equal-sized portions of cabbage on each plate. Slice monkfish into medallions and arrange on top of cabbage. Garnish with fresh parsley.

Cabbage is clearly one of the sturdier vegetables, and it will keep refrigerated for up to six weeks if not cut. Looser heads like Savoy and Napa cabbage should be used within three weeks. Do not wash it before storing, because moisture will bring on decay.

Monkfish Kabobs

The nice thing about making kabobs in the slow cooker is that you don't have to worry about parts or all of them burning on the grill.

Makes 4 to 6 servings.

⅓ cup olive oil

1 tablespoon herbes de Provence

2 cloves garlic, mashed

¼ teaspoon salt

½ teaspoon pepper

2 lbs monkfish, cut into cubes

1 red bell pepper, seeded and cut into large chunks

1 green bell pepper, seeded and cut into large chunks

1 onion, cut into thick wedges

1 zucchini, cut into thin slices

2 quarts ripe cherry tomatoes

Wooden skewers, cut or broken into sizes to fit into the slow cooker

1. In a large bowl, combine the olive oil, herbes, garlic, salt, and pepper, and stir to combine. Add the fish, peppers, onions, and zucchini, and toss to coat all.

2. Put the fish and vegetables onto the skewers, working in the cherry tomatoes. Put the skewers in the slow cooker as you finish them. Pour the remaining dressing over the skewers.

3. Cook on Low for 3 to 4 hours or on High for 2 to 3 hours until fish is cooked through and vegetables are crisp-tender.

Variations:
* Use salmon instead of monkfish.
* Spice it up by adding some cayenne to the dressing, or by including slices of fresh seeded, sliced jalapenos or other hot peppers.

Salmon Cakes

These are so easy to make! Serve with fresh lettuce, tomato, and thinly sliced red onions.

Makes 4 servings.

2 14.5-oz cans cooked salmon

¼ cup oat bran

2 scallions, white parts only, minced fine

½ cup red pepper, minced

½ teaspoon salt

1 teaspoon cayenne pepper

2 eggs

8 tablespoon (1 stick) unsalted butter, melted

1 lemon, cut into wedges

1. Drain the salmon and empty the cans into a large bowl, flaking the meat. Add the oat bran, scallions, red pepper, salt, cayenne, and eggs, and stir to combine. Melt 6 tablespoons of the butter and add to the fish mix, stirring. Form the fish mix into 4 patties.

2. Melt 2 tablespoons of the butter in a skillet and brown the patties on both sides.

3. Transfer to the slow cooker. Cover and cook on Low for 3 to 4 hours until fish is cooked through, turning the cakes midway through. Serve hot with lemon wedges.

Variation:

✳ Vary the flavor by substituting 1 tablespoon of fresh dill, chopped fine, for the teaspoon of cayenne pepper.

Cioppino

This hearty fish stew is made with red wine, in which you can thoroughly indulge for this incredible recipe.

Makes 4 to 6 servings.

¾ lb thick firm-fleshed fish fillets, such as cod, swordfish, or halibut

¼ lb extra-large shrimp

1 dozen crayfish (optional)

3 tablespoons olive oil

2 medium onions, diced

1 red bell pepper, seeds and ribs removed, and finely chopped

2 celery ribs, diced

3 cloves garlic, minced

2 tablespoons fresh oregano, chopped

2 teaspoons fresh thyme

28-oz can diced tomatoes, undrained

1½ cups dry red wine

2 tablespoons tomato paste

1 bay leaf

¼ cup fresh parsley, chopped

3 tablespoons fresh basil, chopped

Salt and pepper to taste

1. Rinse fish and pat dry with paper towels. Remove and discard any skin of bones. Cut fish into 1-inch cubes.

2. Peel and devein the shrimp. Wash the crayfish thoroughly. Refrigerate all seafood until ready to use, tightly covered with plastic wrap.

3. Heat oil in a medium skillet over medium-high heat. Add onions, red bell pepper, celery, garlic, oregano, and thyme. Cook, stirring frequently, for 3 minutes, or until onions are translucent. Scrape mixture into the slow cooker.

4. Add tomatoes, wine, tomato paste, and bay leaf to the slow cooker and stir well to dissolve tomato paste. Cook on Low for 5 to 7 hours or on High for 2 to 3 hours, until vegetables are almost tender.

5. If cooking on Low, raise the heat to High. Add seafood, parsley, and basil. Cook 1 hour or so, or until fish is cooked through. Remove and discard bay leaf, and season to taste with salt and pepper.

Crayfish are one of the few mollusks that don't have carbs. They are popular in Cajun cooking. Resembling mini lobsters, they turn bright red when they're cooked. Getting the flesh out of the shells is a culinary challenge. If they're not available in your area, just do without.

Maryland Crabs

You can imagine you're visiting the Chesapeake Bay area by making crabs seasoned with Old Bay. If you want to get authentic, cover your picnic table with brown paper and pile the crabs on top to eat. When you've picked through the shells, roll up the paper and toss the whole mess.

Makes 4 servings.

2 cups water

½ cup distilled vinegar

¼ cup Old Bay Seasoning

1 tablespoon salt

6 to 8 blue crabs (about 1 lb each)

½ cup unsalted butter, melted

1. In a bowl, mix the water, vinegar, seasoning, and salt until well combined. Pour into the slow cooker. Cover and turn to High.

2. After 1 hour, add the crabs. Cover again and continue to cook on High for about 2 more hours, until crabs have turned bright red and cooked through.

3. Divide the butter into bowls for dipping.

It's so worth the splurge to order Maryland blue crabs online. They arrive super-fresh and ready to cook and eat. What a treat!

Shrimp Creole

The Creole cuisine of Louisiana is an amalgam of French, Italian, and Spanish influences tempered with African-American. Shrimp Creole is one of the premier Creole dishes.

Makes 4 to 6 servings.

3 tablespoon olive oil

6 scallions, white parts and 3 inches of green tops, chopped

2 celery ribs, sliced

½ green bell pepper, seeded and diced

3 cloves garlic, minced

1 tablespoon dried oregano

1 tablespoon paprika

1 teaspoon ground cumin

½ teaspoon dried basil

15-oz can tomato sauce

½ cup white wine

2 bay leaves

1½ lb extra-large shrimp, peeled and deveined

Salt and cayenne to taste

1. Heat oil in a medium skillet over medium-high heat. Add scallions, celery, bell pepper, and garlic. Cook, stirring frequently, for 3 minutes, or until scallions are translucent. Reduce the heat to low, and stir in oregano, paprika, cumin, and basil. Cook for about 1 minute, stirring constantly. Scrape mixture into the slow cooker.

2. Add tomato sauce, wine, and bay leaves to the slow cooker, and stir well. Cook on Low for 4 to 6 hours or on High for 2 to 3 hours, or until vegetables are soft.

3. If cooking on Low, raise the heat to High. Remove and discard bay leaves, and stir in shrimp. Cook for 15 to 30 minutes, or until shrimp are pink and cooked through. Season to taste with salt and cayenne.

Do not equate the words "fresh shrimp" with shrimp that have never been frozen. The truth is you probably would be unable to find never-frozen shrimp fresh from the ocean unless you net it yourself. That's because these days shrimp are harvested, cleaned, and flash-frozen on the boats before they ever reach the shore. But if you plan to freeze shrimp, ask the fishmonger to sell you some still frozen rather than thawed in the case.

Swordfish with Ginger Maple Balsamic

This is another recipe that calls for a sweetener, which is technically forbidden on a low-carb diet. Reserve this recipe for when you've been on the diet for a while. The maple syrup is a great all-natural sweetener that truly complements the other flavors in this dish.

Makes 4 to 6 servings.

4 tablespoons olive oil

3 tablespoons lemon juice

2 cloves garlic, chopped

½ teaspoon salt

½ cup dry white wine

2 lbs swordfish steaks

½ cup balsamic vinegar

1 tablespoon maple syrup (all natural)

1 teaspoon grated ginger (fresh, not dried)

1. In a bowl, combine the olive oil, lemon juice, garlic, salt, and wine. Pour into the slow cooker. Put the swordfish steaks in the cooker. Cover and cook on Low for 4 hours or until the fish is cooked through.

2. Make the sauce on the stove by combining the balsamic, syrup, and ginger in a small saucepan. Bring to a boil then reduce heat to a simmer. Cook until the sauce has been reduced and thickened, about 30 minutes, stirring regularly. If desired to thicken more, sprinkle a very small amount of xanthan in it and whisk. Serve the sauce over the swordfish steaks.

Variation:

✳ This is also delicious with tuna steaks, or even with lobster tails or monkfish. The sweet-salt sauce calls for a firm or substantial piece of fish.

Swordfish with Lemon and Capers

Swordfish is such a wonderfully meaty fish that it stands up to some stronger seasonings, including capers. They add an extra tang to the lemony dish.

Makes 2 to 4 servings.

2 lbs swordfish steaks

2 lemons

Salt and pepper to taste

2 tablespoons capers

2 tablespoons clarified butter

¼ cup fish stock or water

1 tablespoon fresh dill, chopped

1. Put the swordfish steaks on a piece of aluminum foil that will be big enough to wrap over the fish to form a sealed cooking "tent." With the fish in the middle of the piece of foil, squeeze the juice of the lemons over them, removing seeds as you go. Sprinkle the fish with some salt and pepper, the put the capers over it. Cut the butter into small pieces and dot the steaks with it.

2. Bring up the sides of the foil and begin to form the packet. When the sides are up, add the stock or water before securing all edges together and fully enclosing the fish.

3. Put the packet in the slow cooker. Cook on Low for 3 to 4 hours or on High for 2 to 3 hours. It's cooked when the flesh flakes easily but is still moist. Be careful not to overcook. When serving, pour the sauce from the packet over the fish. Garnish with dill.

Swordfish contains no carbohydrates at all. It does contain fats, but the healthy type (mono- and polyunsaturated), which include omega-3 fatty acids.

Lemon-Mustard Bluefish

Tangy and definitely fishy, this is a recipe for people who really enjoy bluefish and want to wake up their taste buds.

Makes 4 to 6 servings.

4 tablespoons unsalted butter

2 tablespoons fresh-squeezed lemon juice

2 teaspoons Dijon mustard

¼ teaspoon salt

2 lbs bluefish filets

4 tablespoon fresh parsley, chopped

1. In a microwave-safe measuring cup, melt the butter. Add the lemon juice, mustard, and salt, and stir to combine.

2. Pour the sauce into the slow cooker to coat the bottom. Place the filets on the sauce.

3. Cover and cook on Low for 3 to 4 hours, until fish is cooked through. Garnish with parsley when serving.

Bluefish are common along the eastern seaboard between April (in warmer climates) and into September for cooler climates. Full-grown, they are about 7 inches long and weigh about 20 pounds. They are named for their blue coloring, which fades to a white belly. Fast-moving and aggressive, bluefish travel in schools and can often be located off the shores by agitation in the water.

Fish Veracruz

People seem to lose sight of the fact that most of Mexico is bounded by coastline because so much of our beloved Tex-Mex food is based on dishes from landlocked Sonora province. This delicate fish in a spicy sauce is wonderful on its own or in a lettuce wrap.

Makes 4 to 6 servings.

2 tablespoons olive oil

2 onions, thinly sliced

4 cloves garlic, minced

1 jalapeno or Serrano pepper, seeds and ribs removed, finely chopped (wear rubber gloves to do this)

1 tablespoon chili powder

2 teaspoons dried oregano

14.5-oz can diced tomatoes, undrained

1 cup white wine

2 tablespoons freshly squeezed lemon juice

2 tablespoons tomato paste

1 teaspoon grated lemon zest

¼ cup sliced green olives (packed in oil or water with no additional chemicals)

1½ lbs cod or halibut, cut into serving pieces

Salt and pepper to taste

1. Heat oil in a medium skillet over medium-high heat. Add onions, garlic, and pepper. Cook, stirring frequently, for 3 minutes, or until onion is translucent. Reduce the heat to low, and stir in chili powder and oregano. Cook for 1 minute, stirring constantly. Scrape mixture into the slow cooker.

2. Add tomatoes, wine, lemon juice, tomato paste, and lemon zest to the slow cooker, and stir well. Cook for 4 to 6 hours on Low, or 2 to 3 hours on High, until vegetables are tender.

3. If cooking on Low, raise the heat to High and cook for an additional 25 to 35 minutes, or until fish is cooked through and flakes easily. Season with salt and pepper.

Chili powder is a premixed blend of herbs and spices. If you make it yourself, you can personalize the taste to suit your own. The base should be ground red chiles and ground cumin. Then add as much paprika, ground coriander, cayenne, and oregano as you like. Some brands also include garlic powder and some onion.

Rare Salmon with Salsa Topping

The slight rare finish of this dish leaves the fish succulent and tasty, with the perfect strength of flavor for the fresh "salsa" topping.

Makes 4 to 6 servings.

4 to 6 salmon steaks (about 6 oz each), at least ¾-inch thick

3 tablespoons olive oil

3 cloves garlic, minced

2 tablespoons ground cumin

2 tablespoons chili powder

Salt and pepper to taste

4 ripe plum tomatoes, cored, seeded, and chopped

¼ cup red onion, chopped fine

2 tablespoons fresh-squeezed lime juice

1. Rub salmon with 1 tablespoon of the oil. Combine garlic, cumin, chili powder, salt and pepper in a small bowl. Rub mixture on both sides of the salmon.

2. Combine remaining oil with tomatoes, onion, and lime juice.

3. Place salmon in the slow cooker. Cook on High for about 40 minutes. Turn salmon gently with a slotted spatula. Top salmon with the tomato mixture, and cook on High for an additional 20 to 30 minutes for rare, or longer for fish that is better done.

Many of the thick, firm-fleshed fish like salmon, halibut, cod, tilapia, and flounder, can be purchased frozen. It's handy to keep a supply of fish fillets in your freezer. Dethawing them so they don't lose flavor or texture is the secret to successful recipes. We've found the best way is to put individual fillets in plastic baggies with air-tight seals, and then submerse in a bowl of cool (not warm!) water. It only takes about 15 minutes to thaw. Or put the frozen fillets in the refrigerator for several hours.

Brook Trout *Italiano*

The combination of oregano, basil, parsley, garlic, and rosemary make for a fragrant, delicious, and nutritious topping to this tender fish.

Makes 4 servings.

3 to 4 lbs brook trout fillets

¼ cup olive oil

2 cloves garlic, minced

1 teaspoon fresh oregano, chopped, or ¼ teaspoon dried

1 teaspoon fresh basil, chopped, or ½ teaspoon dried

1 teaspoon fresh parsley, chopped, or ½ teaspoon dried

1 teaspoon fresh rosemary, chopped, or ½ teaspoon dried

Juice of 1 lemon

¼ cup dry white wine

1. Place the fillets in the slow cooker. Add the garlic to the olive oil, and drizzle over the fish.

2. In a small bowl, combine the herbs and mix with a fork to blend without overly crushing. Sprinkle the herb mixture over the fish. Squeeze the lemon over the fish and add the wine.

3. Cook on Low for about 2 hours or on High for about 1 hour. The herbs will have made a thin carpet over the fish. Pour the juices from the cooker over the fish when serving. Season with salt and pepper.

It's easy to make your own Italian seasonings blend to have handy for seasoning fish, poultry, sauces, and even sprinkling on salads. Using dried herbs, combine 1 tablespoon each of the oregano, basil, parsley, and rosemary. Substitute 2 teaspoons garlic powder for the fresh garlic. Store in a small glass jar with an airtight lid.

Brook Trout with Lemon

This recipe calls for cooking the fish whole, but don't worry—filleting it when it's cooked is easy. It makes an elegant presentation on the plate, and there's something very satisfying about removing the skeleton yourself.

Makes 2 to 4 servings.

2 medium to large whole brook trout, cleaned by the fishmonger but not filleted

2 lemons

2 teaspoon herbes de Provence

Salt to taste

2 tablespoons clarified butter

⅔ cup dry white wine

1 tablespoon fresh parsley, chopped

1. Put 1 trout each on pieces of aluminum foil that are big enough to wrap over the fish to form a sealed cooking "tent." With the trout in the middle of the piece of foil, squeeze the juice of 1 lemon over each, removing seeds as you go. Sprinkle each fish with a teaspoon of herbes de Provence and some salt. Cut the butter into 4 small pieces and place two pats each on top of the fish. If desired, slice the lemons and place 2 slices in the cavity inside each fish.

2. Bring up the sides of the foil and begin to form the packet. When the sides are up, pour ⅓ cup wine on each trout before securing all edges together and fully enclosing the fish.

3. Put the trout packets in the slow cooker. Cook on Low for 2 to 3 hours or on High for 1 to 2 hours. Halfway through, peek into one of the packets to see how the fish is doing. It's cooked when the flesh is pale and easily flakes away from the bones. Make sure it's cooked through before removing from packets and serving. Serve whole, pouring the sauce in the packet over the fish. Garnish with parsley.

Removing the trout's skeleton so your fish is free of bones is easy if you take your time. With the fish on your plate, loosen the flesh close to the spine and gently scrape/slide the top "fillet" off the skeleton. When it's off and half the skeleton is exposed, lift the head or tail of the trout and gently pull back and lift up to pull the remaining skeleton away from the fillet on the bottom. Discard the skeleton.

Salmon with Spinach

This is a great throw-together meal for busy households because you can use frozen salmon fillets. Thaw them by placing each fillet in an air-tight plastic baggie and submersing in a bowl of cool water. It takes about 20 minutes to thaw several fillets at once.

Makes 2 to 4 servings.

4 16-oz bags fresh baby spinach greens (or a spinach/kale combo)

2 cloves garlic, minced

2 tablespoons olive oil

4 frozen salmon fillets, thawed

Salt to taste

2 tablespoons toasted sesame seeds

1. Working in batches, put spinach in the colander and give it a quick rinse, picking through the leaves and removing any large stems. Shake excess water from the spinach, but don't dry thoroughly. Put spinach in slow cooker after rinsing. When all spinach is in the slow cooker, add the garlic and oil and stir to combine and coat the leaves.

2. Place the salmon fillets on top of the spinach greens. Cook on Low for about 1 hour, until spinach is wilted and fish is cooked through. Depending on how well done you like your salmon, you may want to cook it an additional 15 to 20 minutes.

3. In a small, dry skillet over medium-high heat, add the sesame seeds and cook, shaking lightly or stirring to keep the seeds from sticking and burning, until seeds are lightly toasted, about 2 minutes. Garnish salmon and spinach with the sesame seeds, and season with salt to taste.

Toasting seeds and nuts is a way to bring out their rich flavors. In this recipe, when the seeds are toasted, you could toss them in 1 tablespoon of sesame oil for even more sesame goodness.

Fish with Olives

The secret to this recipe is to chop the olives fine so that you have a tapenade. The flavors blend better with the fish as it cooks.

Makes 4 servings.

¼ cup unsalted butter, melted

1 lb white fish filets (sea bass, halibut, sole, or tilapia)

¼ cup mixed olives gourmet olives, pitted and chopped

1 tablespoon balsamic vinegar

1 teaspoon raw honey

Salt and pepper

1. Pour the melted butter into the slow cooker so it coats the bottom.

2. Place the filets on the butter. Season with salt and pepper.

3. In a small bowl, combine the olives, balsamic vinegar, and honey. Scoop the mixture over the fish.

4. Cover and cook on Low for 3 to 4 hours until the fish is cooked through.

Olives are rich in phytonutrients like flavonoids and phenols, which have antioxidant properties.

Chapter 7

Low-Carb Vegetable and Side Dishes

While on a low-carb diet, you can't go to the fresh or frozen vegetable section of your supermarket or even to your farmer's market and choose just anything. There are, in fact, vegetables with high carb contents. These include potatoes, sweet potatoes, yams, peas, and even green beans. While you do have to keep your carb-counting wits about you, there are certainly plenty of delicious fresh vegetables from which to choose. These include all leafy greens, broccoli, cauliflower, Brussels sprouts, celery, eggplant, tomatoes, yellow squash and zucchini, mushrooms, peppers, radishes, fennel, and thankfully, garlic, onions, and ginger. The recipes in this chapter all feature combinations of these, slow-cooked to earthy goodness.

Garlic Mashed Cauliflower

This super-simple recipe produces such a flavorful and creamy dish that you will not miss traditional mashed potatoes loaded with butter or sour cream. Enjoy!

Makes 6 to 8 servings.

2 14-oz bags of frozen cauliflower florets
Hot water to cover
1 small head of garlic, roasted
1 tablespoon unsalted butter
Salt and pepper to taste

1. Put the cauliflower in the slow cooker and add hot tap water until the florets are just covered. Cover and cook on Low for 4 to 5 hours or on High for 2 to 3 hours until cauliflower is tender.

2. While the cauliflower is cooking in the slow cooker, roast the garlic. To do this, preheat the oven to 400F. Peel off the outermost layers of skin on a whole clove of garlic, and cut off about ¼ to ½ inch from the top so the cloves are exposed. Put the head on a baking pan (like a muffin tin or cake pan), and drizzle about a teaspoon of olive oil on the top, being sure to coat it. Cover with aluminum foil and bake for about 30 to 40 minutes. Allow to cool before squeezing out cloves.

3. Drain the cauliflower and put it in a bowl. Add the roasted garlic cloves and the oil, and mash with a potato masher or puree with an immersion blender, mashing to desired consistency. Season with salt and pepper.

The slow cooker helps break down cauliflower so that it is easy to mash. Serve mashed cauliflower as a side or as a base for other vegetable or meat dishes.

Braised Fennel

Fennel has an almost silky texture and sweet flavor once it's braised, and this dish goes with almost anything and everything, especially dishes with dark colors and assertive seasonings.

Makes 4 to 6 servings.

2 medium fennel bulbs, about 1 lb each

2 tablespoons butter

½ small onion, thinly sliced

1 clove garlic, minced

1 cup chicken broth

1 teaspoon fresh thyme, or ¼ teaspoon dried

Salt and pepper to taste

1. Cut stalks off fennel bulb, trim root end, and cut bulb in half through the root. Trim out core, then slice fennel into 1-inch-thick slices across the bulb. Arrange slices in the slow cooker, and repeat with second bulb.

2. Heat butter in a small skillet over medium heat. Add onion and garlic and cook, stirring frequently, for 3 minutes, or until onion is translucent. Scrape mixture into the slow cooker.

3. Add broth and thyme to the slow cooker. Cook on Low for 4 to 6 hours or on High for 2 to 3 hours, or until fennel is tender. Season to taste with salt and pepper.

Although the celery-like stalks are trimmed off the fennel bulb for this dish, don't throw them out. They add a wonderful anise flavor as well as a crisp texture and are used in place of celery in salads and other raw dishes.

Roasted Tomatoes

Because the slow cooker retains the moisture in foods, these won't need to cook long to become moist and flavorful. Seasoned with some herbs and garlic, they make a colorful and tasty side dish.

Makes 2 to 4 servings.

4 large, ripe tomatoes, cut in half, seeds removed

2 cloves garlic, minced

1 teaspoon fresh oregano, minced, or ½ teaspoon dried

1 teaspoon fresh parsley, chopped

Salt and pepper to taste

1. Place cut tomatoes bottom down in the slow cooker. Sprinkle minced garlic on top, then sprinkle with the oregano.

2. Cover and cook on Low for 3 to 4 hours or on High for 1 to 2 hours. Season with salt and pepper, and garnish with the parsley.

Summer-ripe tomatoes taste too good to cook: Use them in salads, salsas, or to stuff with some meat or vegetable mix. Slow cooking is great for off-season tomatoes, preferably vine-ripened.

Curried Vegetables

When you're looking forward to coming home and putting a piece of meat on the grill, you'll also be glad to have prepared this in the morning so you can have it as a side dish. The flavors are incredible.

Makes 4 to 6 servings.

2 cups broccoli florets

2 cups cauliflower florets

1 eggplant, cubed

6 or 7 radishes, scrubbed, trimmed, and halved

1 teaspoon curry powder

1 teaspoon cumin

½ teaspoon turmeric

½ teaspoon cayenne pepper

½ teaspoon salt

14.5-oz can diced tomatoes

Fresh coriander for garnish

1. In a large bowl, combine the broccoli, cauliflower, eggplant, and radishes. Add each of the spices, and stir well to combine and to coat the vegetables with the seasonings. Transfer the vegetables to the slow cooker. Add the tomatoes.

2. Cover and cook on Low for 6 to 8 hours or on High for 4 to 5 hours, until the vegetables are tender. Season with additional salt and pepper if desired, and garnish with fresh coriander.

Variation:

✱ For some variety and to add crunch to the dish when it's cooked, substitute unsweetened coconut for the coriander as the garnish. Curry dishes are traditionally served with a selection of sides, ranging from spicy to savory to sweet (think chutney), so the coconut is a refreshing choice.

Zucchini, Tomato, and Leek Gratin

This is a fabulous dish to make in late summer when these vegetables are plentiful and bursting with goodness and just-picked flavor.

Makes 4 to 6 servings.

3 tablespoons olive oil

3 or 4 cloves garlic, minced

2 medium leeks, white parts only, thinly sliced

12 oz shredded cheddar cheese

⅓ cup grated Parmesan cheese

1 teaspoon Italian seasonings

1 egg, beaten

1 large zucchini, thinly sliced

6 fresh basil leaves

3 lbs fresh tomatoes, sliced, seeds removed

Salt and pepper to taste

1. Spray the inside of the slow cooker with non-stick cooking spray.

2. Heat the oil over medium-high heat and cook the garlic and leeks, stirring, for about 5 minutes, until softened. Remove from heat.

3. In a bowl, combine the cheddar, Parmesan, Italian seasonings, and beaten egg. Mix well.

4. Make a layer of zucchini on the bottom of the slow cooker. Top with some of the leek mixture, slices of tomatoes, a few basil leaves, and a portion of the cheese mixture. Repeat the layers, finishing with the cheese mixture. There should be 3 or 4 layers.

5. Cover and cook on Low for 4 to 5 hours or on High for 3 to 4 hours. Season with salt and pepper.

If you don't have leeks, the dish tastes fine without them (better with, of course, but still great). When making the layers in the slow cooker, add some thin slices of garlic on top of the tomatoes before putting on the basil leaves.

Sardinian-Style Cabbage

This cabbage dish is subtly flavored with pancetta and herbs, and the braising makes it a tender treat for any winter meal.

Makes 6 to 8 servings.

2 tablespoons olive oil

¼ lb pancetta, diced

2 cloves garlic, minced

1 large head (1½ lbs) green cabbage, shredded

2 tablespoons fresh chopped parsley

1 bay leaf

1 cup chicken stock or broth

Salt and pepper to taste

1. Heat oil in a large skillet over medium-high heat. Add pancetta, stirring frequently, and cook for 4 to 5 minutes, or until browned. Add garlic, and cook for 30 seconds, stirring constantly. Add cabbage, parsley, bay leaf, and stock, and bring to a boil. Scrape mixture into the slow cooker.

2. Cook on Low for 5 to 7 hours or on High for 2 to 3 hours, or until cabbage softens. Remove and discard bay leaf, season to taste with salt and pepper.

> An advantage of cooking cruciferous vegetables such as cabbage, cauliflower, or broccoli in the slow cooker is that the house doesn't smell like vegetables for days, which many people find offensive. This is because very little liquid evaporates from the slow cooker, and it's the steam in the air that carries the fragrance.

Roasted Radishes

It turns out that roasted radishes can taste almost like potatoes—except better! These are delicious finished in the oven, too, to give them a bit of a "skin."

Makes 4 to 6 servings.

4 cups radishes, quartered

4 tablespoons butter

1 teaspoon sea salt

1 tablespoon chopped chives (or other fresh herb)

Salt and pepper to taste

1. Put the radishes in the slow cooker. Dot with small pieces of the butter and sprinkle with the sea salt. Cover and cook on Low for about 6 hours, turning occasionally. Increase the heat to High for about 30 to 40 minutes.

2. If desired, spread the cooked radishes on a baking sheet and put them under the broiler in the oven for just a couple of minutes a side.

3. Serve with additional butter and chopped chives, and season with additional salt and pepper.

These are a yummy snack that are also delicious dipped in a seasoned sour cream spread or a no-sugar-added salad dressing.

Spicy Kale

This is a versatile and easy side dish to prepare. It is a great accompaniment to everything from meats to seafood to other vegetable dishes.

Makes about 1 ½ cups.

1½ lbs kale

¼ cup olive oil

4 cloves garlic, minced

½ to ¾ teaspoon crushed red pepper flakes

¾ cup vegetable broth

Salt to taste

1. Rinse kale and discard thick ribs and stems. Cut kale into ½-inch slices.

2. Heat oil in a deep saucepan over medium-high heat. Add garlic and crushed red pepper flakes and cook for about 30 seconds, stirring constantly. Add kale a few handfuls at a time, and stir. Cover the pan for 30 seconds, and then stir again. Continue until all kale is wilted. Scrape kale into the slow cooker.

3. Add broth to the slow cooker, and stir well. Cover and cook on Low for 3 to 4 hours or on High for 1 to 2 hours.

4. Uncover and cook kale for an additional 30 to 45 minutes, or until very tender. Season with salt.

Variation:

✳ Substitute Swiss chard or collard greens if desired—or do a combination of them.

Kale is the renegade cousin of the cabbage family. Its flavor is very mild, and it has frilly, deep green leaves that look like a bouquet of flowers rather than a tight head.

Eggplant Parmesan

When you make this as a side dish, you won't miss bread, or potatoes, or even dessert! It's filling, delicious, and great in every way.

Makes 4 servings.

1 large eggplant

3 tablespoons salt

32-oz jar of no-sugar-added marinara sauce

2 cloves garlic, pressed

1 teaspoon oregano

1 teaspoon dried rosemary

12 oz fresh mozzarella

1 cup grated Parmesan cheese

1. Prepare the eggplant, by slicing it into ¼-inch rounds, discarding the ends. Place paper towels on a baking sheet and put the slices on them. Sprinkle liberally with salt. Turn the rounds after 10 minutes and put salt on the other side of the slices. The salt draws out the moisture. After at least 10 minutes with salt on each side, blot the slices as dry as possible.

2. Empty the jar of marinara into a bowl. Press the garlic into the sauce and add the oregano and rosemary. Stir to combine.

3. Begin to layer the eggplant Parmesan. The layers will be sauce, eggplant, mozzarella, and Parmesan. Start with marinara and build up, ending with a layer of Parmesan cheese.

4. Cover and cook on Low for 4 hours until the eggplant is cooked through and the cheese is melted.

There are lots of ways to kick up this recipe. Consider using different kinds of grated hard cheese to combine with the Parmesan, like Asiago or aged cheddar. Add cayenne or red pepper flakes to the marinara sauce. Try a low-carb cream sauce instead of marinara, and supplement with different herbs.

Artichokes with Lemon and Herbs

This vegetable can be intimidating because they are spiky and can take a long time to cook when steamed. The slow cooker is the perfect way to prepare artichokes. Set them in the cooker and come home to perfectly cooked artichokes.

Makes 4 to 6 servings.

4 to 6 artichokes, depending on size of vegetables and the slow cooker

1 lemon, quartered

3 cloves garlic, crushed

1 teaspoon fresh rosemary, minced

2 cups water

1. Wash and pat dry the artichokes. Trim the stem to about ¼ inch from bottom. Pull off the first couple of layers of leaves at the bottom, and snip the pointy ends off the leaves all around the chokes.

2. Place the artichokes in the slow cooker, bottoms down. Squeeze the juice of the lemons over the artichokes and put the squeezed quarters in with the artichokes, distributed throughout. Peel the garlic cloves and crush with the back of a knife. Put the garlic cloves in the slow cooker, distributed throughout. Sprinkle the rosemary around the artichokes.

3. Pour the water around the artichokes so that it covers the bottom of the slow cooker with about ½ to 1 inch of water. Cover and cook on Low for 6 to 8 hours or on High for 4 to 5 hours. Artichokes should be tender, with leaves easily breaking away from the core. Serve hot or at room temperature with the lemon/garlic juice as a dipping sauce for the leaves.

Artichokes are a lot of fun to eat as you work your way through the leaves to what is considered the vegetable's most delicious part, its heart. Peel each leaf off and dip the bottom into the lemon/garlic cooking liquid. Put the leaf in your mouth, press down with your teeth, and scrape the tender flesh from the lower part of the leaves. Work through the artichoke until the leaves are small and nearly transparent. Pull off the last tip of leaves. The heart will be left, attached to the stem. There is some "fuzz" on the top of the heart that needs to be gently scraped off, as it can be bitter. It falls off easily. Now enjoy the heart!

Simply Spinach

The joy of this recipe is that you can use bags of frozen spinach and know that, hours later, it'll be just the right consistency.

Serves 6 to 8.

2 tablespoons olive oil

3 cloves garlic, minced

2 32-oz bags of frozen spinach

Salt and pepper to taste

1. Heat the oil in a skillet and sauté the garlic over medium heat for about 2 minutes. Put the frozen spinach in the slow cooker and drizzle the garlic-oil mixture over it.

2. Cover and cook on Low for 4 to 6 hours, stirring about halfway through to help distribute heat. Season with salt and pepper before serving.

Variation:

* Experiment with mixing frozen leafy greens, using one bag of spinach and one bag of another vegetable like collard greens or kale (also frozen). Add some sesame oil at the end for some nutty flavor if desired.

Brussels Sprouts with Pancetta

Chopping the Brussels sprouts reduces the overall cooking time and retains some additional flavor. The pancetta is a nice, thick bacon, but you can substitute thick-cut regular bacon.

Makes 4 to 6 servings.

1 lb Brussels sprouts

6 slices Pancetta, cut into 1-inch pieces

3 cloves garlic, minced

½ onion, diced

¼ cup chicken broth or white wine

Salt and pepper to taste

1. Trim the Brussels sprouts of tough ends and damaged outer leaves. Quarter or chop the sprouts into a chunky "slaw."

2. Cook the Pancetta over medium heat (not too high) until just crisp. Transfer the cooked bits to a plate covered with a paper towel to drain. In the fat from the meat, sauté the garlic and onions for about 2 minutes.

3. Put the Brussels sprouts in the slow cooker. Top with the onion/garlic mixture and ½ of the Pancetta. Pour the wine over everything. Cover and cook on Low for 4 to 6 hours, or on High for about 3 hours. Before serving, stir in additional Pancetta bits. Season with salt and pepper.

> Pancetta is Italian bacon. It is cut thicker than American bacon and has less fat. If you can't find it or simply prefer to use bacon, the dish will be smokier and saltier overall.

Kale and Bacon

The bacon does double-duty in this recipe, not only adding crunchy flavor bites once the kale is cooked but providing a nice fat base in which to prep the greens.

Makes 4 to 6 servings.

6 pieces of bacon, chopped

2 lbs curly kale, tough stems removed and coarsely chopped

1 onion, diced

Salt and pepper to taste

1. Put bacon in a skillet and heat to medium high. Cook bacon pieces until browned and just getting crisp, transferring cooked pieces to a plate covered with a paper towel. Set bacon aside.

2. Put onion in bacon fat and cook, stirring, for about 2 minutes until onion is translucent. Add kale to skillet and cook, stirring, until kale is just coated with bacon fat, about 2 minutes. Transfer kale and onions to the slow cooker. Cook on Low for 2 hours or on High for about 1 hour.

3. When kale is cooked through, transfer to a bowl. Stir in the cooked bacon bits and serve.

Variation:

❋ The kale in this recipe can be substituted for collards, Swiss chard, sorrel, and even full grown spinach (not baby spinach leaves).

Basic Broccoli

When you want all the goodness of this delicious vegetable, here's what to do.

Makes 4 to 6 servings.

2 lbs broccoli

½ cup water

2 tablespoons olive oil

Salt and pepper to taste

1. Prepare broccoli by breaking off the florets and putting them in a colander. With the tougher stem, cut off the bottom that has the toughest part. With a sharp knife, separate the hard "skin" from the more tender center of the stem. Cut the remaining broccoli into large chunks. Rinse all the pieces in the colander and shake vigorously to remove as much water as possible.

2. Put the broccoli in the slow cooker and add the water. Drizzle with the oil, and sprinkle some salt and pepper on the broccoli. Cover and cook on Low for 2 to 3 hours or on High for 1 to 2 hours.

An easy and interesting addition to the cooked broccoli is a sprinkle of coconut aminos. They give a hint of Chinese flavor to the greens.

Warm Salad

On a cold day it's nice to have a warm salad. It's so easy to do with a slow cooker!

Makes 6 servings.

1 bag baby spinach leaves

1 bag kale

1 bag Italian salad greens (that includes radicchio and endive)

3 scallions

2 tablespoons olive oil

1 tablespoon balsamic vinegar

Salt and pepper to taste

6 slices bacon (optional)

1. Go through the bags of greens and trim them of excess stems or tough middles. Combine all greens in a large bowl. Peel off the outside layer of the scallions; trim the rooted end and most of the green part. Slice thin and add to the leaves. Stir in the olive oil.

2. Put the oiled greens into the slow cooker. Cover and cook on Low for about 1 hour until the greens are wilted. Stir in the balsamic vinegar and season with salt and pepper.

3. If desired, cook the bacon in the microwave to crispy. When serving the salad, sprinkle with the bacon.

> This is also a great way to finish up bags of greens that can accumulate in your fridge. Supplement with other vegetables, too.

Slow and Stewy Mushrooms

Mushrooms are one of those vegetables that you can slow-cook for nearly forever so long as you keep an eye on the liquid. The longer they cook, the better they taste.

Makes 4 to 6 servings.

2 lbs mushrooms, preferably a mix of button, crimini, and Portobello

¼ cup olive oil

1 cup beef stock or broth

Salt and pepper to taste

1. Clean the mushrooms by wiping away dirt with a soft cloth or mushroom brush. Remove the toughest part of the stems, and slice into thick slices/chunks.

2. Heat the oil over medium heat in a large skillet and add the mushrooms. Stir to coat with the oil and cook, stirring for about 5 minutes.

3. Transfer the mushrooms to the slow cooker, add the beef stock, sprinkle with salt and pepper, and stir to combine. Cover and cook on Low for 7 to 9 hours, or on High for 5 to 6 hours. Stir once during cooking to be sure there is enough liquid, which there should be. For the last 30 minutes of cooking, turn to High and remove the lid. This will cook the mushroom broth down a bit to make the dish slightly thicker.

> These slow-cooked mushrooms are the perfect accompaniment to steak. Mmm!

Ratatouille

Each Mediterranean country has its own take on the primary ingredients in this classic late-summer dish. We like to give them all a shot, and settled on this one for the slow cooker.

Makes 6 to 8 servings.

2 medium-sized eggplants, cubed

1 large zucchini, cubed

3 green peppers, seeded and cubed

6 large, ripe tomatoes, seeds removed and coarsely chopped

2 onions, chopped

6 cloves garlic, minced

¼ cup olive oil

1. In a large bowl, combine the eggplant, zucchini, peppers, and tomatoes. Stir to mix well. Put vegetables in the slow cooker.

2. Top with chopped onions and minced garlic, and add the olive oil over everything. Cover and cook on Low for 4 to 5 hours or on High for 2 to 3 hours until the eggplant is tender and vegetables are melded.

The general consensus is that ratatouille is a dish originating in Nice in the south of France. It is a "stew" made with tomatoes, eggplant, peppers, zucchini, onions, garlic, and a variety of herbs. The name is thought to derive from the French word touiller, meaning to toss.

Asparagus with Prosciutto

These asparagus spears wrapped in Italian ham are delicious and fun to eat.

Makes 6 to 8 servings.

1 lb asparagus

1 lb pancetta, sliced very thin

1 tablespoon clarified butter or ghee, melted

1. Wash and dry asparagus spears, trimming off tough bottoms by about an inch.

2. Wrap each spear in a slice of prosciutto, and lay the spears gently and carefully in the slow cooker. Drizzle the spears with the melted butter. Cover and cook on Low for about 2 hours or on High for about 1 hour, until spears are tender.

3. Turn heat to High and cook for an additional 15 to 20 minutes with the lid propped open with the handle of a wooden spoon to allow steam to escape. This will dry-crisp the pancetta somewhat.

While thin spears are usually more desirable for quick cooking when steaming asparagus, for this recipe it is preferable to select fatter spears so there is more inside the wrap of prosciutto.

Stewed Peppers

Make a big pot of these when you're planning a picnic. They are the perfect accompaniment to grilled meats ranging from sausage to pork chops to steak to burgers.

Makes 8 to 10 servings.

3 large green peppers, seeds and ribs removed, cut into long slices

2 large red peppers, seeds and ribs removed, cut into long slices

2 large orange peppers, seeds and ribs removed, cut into long slices

1 small head garlic, cloves separated and peeled

½ cup extra virgin olive oil

Salt and pepper to taste

1. Put the pepper slices in the slow cooker. Spread the garlic cloves over the slices. Pour the oil over everything, and season with salt and pepper.

2. Cover and cook on Low for 6 to 8 hours or on High for 4 to 5 hours, until peppers and garlic are tender.

Variation:

✳ Spice up the peppers by adding 1 fresh jalapeno to the other peppers. Remove the seeds and ribs from the jalapeno(s), too, but wear gloves so you don't get the oils on your fingers and then into your eyes.

Mustardy Brussels Sprouts

Slow cooking this earthy veggie mellows its tanginess but brings out its woodsy depth of flavor. A touch of mustard, and seasoning with just a hint of sea salt, add the perfect finish.

Makes 4 to 6 servings.

1 lb Brussels sprouts

3 tablespoons olive oil

1 teaspoon dry mustard

Pinch of sea salt

1. Wash and trim the Brussels sprouts, cutting off the coarsest part of the bottom and a layer or so of the leaves on the bottom. Cut the sprouts in half and put them in the slow cooker.

2. In a measuring cup, mix the olive oil with the dry mustard. Pour over the Brussels sprouts. Cover and cook on Low for 3 to 4 hours or on High for 2 to 3 hours. Before serving, add a pinch of sea salt.

Variation:

* Mustard adds a wonderful tanginess to this recipe, but you can substitute other spices to get different flavors. For spicier sprouts, add some cayenne pepper or Asian chili sauce; for an Indian taste, add hints of curry or cumin.

Classic Collards

This is a variation on the dish that's a staple in the Southern United States. Instead of a ham hock, this recipe uses smoked bacon to add the salty meat flavor that's essential to the dish.

Makes 2 to 4 servings.

1 lb smoked bacon, cut into 1-inch pieces

4 cups water

3 lbs fresh collard greens, rinsed, tough stems removed

1 teaspoon crushed red pepper flakes

2 tablespoons olive oil

Salt and pepper to taste

1. Put the bacon in the slow cooker and add the water. Cover and cook on High for about 1 hour, until liquid is at a boil.

2. Reduce heat to Low and add collard greens, pepper flakes, and oil. Cook on Low for 2 to 3 hours, until greens are tender and flavors are melded. Season with salt and pepper.

Variation:

✳ In lieu of collard greens, you can use Swiss chard, sorrel, and even dandelion greens or a combination of these plus collards.

Cauliflower and Broccoli Au Gratin

Combining these two vegetables adds color, texture, and flavor to a classic comfort-food dish.

Makes 4 to 6 servings.

2 cups cauliflower florets

2 cups broccoli florets

½ cup half-and-half

½ teaspoon dry mustard

¼ teaspoon cayenne

1 teaspoon salt

Freshly ground pepper

1 cup shredded Swiss cheese

1. In a large bowl, combine the cauliflower and broccoli florets. In a smaller bowl, mix the half-and-half, mustard, cayenne, salt, pepper, and cheese.

2. Spray the slow cooker with non-stick spray. Add the vegetables. Pour the cheese sauce over the vegetables. Cover and cook on Low for 6 to 8 hours or on High for 3 to 4 hours.

> Most au gratin dishes contain bread crumbs or a bread filler of some kind. This low-carb recipe does not, but no worries. The delicious result doesn't need the extra filler.

Summer Squash and Herbs

There are all kinds of squash you can use in this recipe, including zucchini, yellow squash, and pattypan. Even spaghetti squash!

Makes 4 servings.

4 small assorted summer squash, or your choice

¼ cup olive oil

1 teaspoon fresh thyme

1 teaspoon fresh rosemary

Salt and pepper to taste

Parmesan cheese, if desired

1. Remove the ends or stems of the squash types you're using, and slice the rest. Put the squash in the slow cooker. Pour the olive oil over it, sprinkle with the herbs, and season with salt and pepper.

2. Cover and cook on Low for about 4 hours, or on High for about 2. Season with additional salt and pepper if desired, and sprinkle with Parmesan if desired.

Pattypan is a summer squash that is small, round, and shallow, with scalloped edges. It's believed to derive from its French name, pâttison, which is a word for a cake made in a scalloped mold. It's grown the world over and comes in green, yellow, and white varieties. It's best eaten when it's still young and tender.

Broccoli Rabe

Consider this your "lazy" way to great broccoli rabe. Compile your ingredients, put them in the slow cooker, and come back many hours later to something truly delicious. The longer this slow cooks, the better, and if you put it on warm after 8 hours, it can go a few more hours.

Makes 4 to 6 servings.

1 lb broccoli rabe
6 large cloves garlic, sliced
1 teaspoon red pepper flakes
⅓ cup extra virgin olive oil
Salt to taste

1. Prepare the broccoli rabe by removing the tough stems and setting aside only the tops and the tender parts of the stems. Put these in a colander and rinse, then spin and/or pat dry.

2. Put the broccoli rabe in the slow cooker, add the garlic, red pepper flakes, and olive oil. Cover and cook on Low for 6 to 8 hours. Do not cook on High. Season with salt to taste.

> Broccoli rabe is related to broccoli and is a member of the turnip family. It is definitely more bitter than broccoli and has long been popular in Italy and Portugal.

Citrusy Asparagus

Hints of lemon and orange in this dish keep the sunshine of spring in this seasonal vegetable.

Makes 4 to 6 servings.

1 lb asparagus, tough parts of stems removed

Zest of one orange (no juice)

2 tablespoons fresh-squeezed lemon juice

¼ cup olive oil

¼ red onion, minced

1 teaspoon fresh tarragon, minced

Salt and pepper to taste

1. Put asparagus in the slow cooker.

2. Zest one of the oranges, then cut the white peel and pith away from the segments. Put the zest and segments in a bowl, and cut the other orange in half, squeezing its juice into the bowl. Add the fresh-squeezed lemon juice, olive oil, onions, and oregano. Pour the fruit juice mixture over the asparagus.

3. Cover and cook on Low for 2 to 3 hours until spears are tender. Season with salt and pepper.

Variation:
* Use the herb lemon balm instead of tarragon.

Chapter 8

Fresh and Simple Desserts

ere's where reality strikes hard, because few ingredients normally associated with dessert—sweet treats—qualify as low carb. Cakes and cookies are out because they include grains (even gluten-free grains have carbs). Many fruits, including apples, mango, bananas, and peaches, are high in carbohydrates. There are low-carb cookbooks available that list dessert recipes, and you can find processed foods in stores that claim to be low-carb desserts. The reason you won't find those in this cookbook is that we believe that artificial sweeteners are not the answer to long-term nutritional health. Studies have shown that artificial sweeteners actually lead to cravings for more sweets, and what's the benefit of that? You're trying hard enough to lose weight for health purposes on a low-carb diet. If you crave sweets, you will fall fast and fall hard. This is something you'll have to be on the lookout for all the time.

Now here's the good news. Do you like butter and cream? They are the pillars of many a decadent dessert, and you can make good use of them in your experiments. Chocolate? That's okay, too (so long as it's unsweetened). And here's another great discovery: 1 teaspoon of all-natural maple sugar (dehydrated maple syrup) has just 2.7 grams of carbs. I added it to a few of the recipes here, but most are flavored with extracts, herbs, and even spices.

Here's the list of low-carb-allowed ingredients that can be combined for desserts:

Dairy

* Butter
* Cream
* Cream cheese
* Half-and-half
* Unsweetened Greek yogurt

Fruits

* Apricot
* Avocado
* Blueberries
* Blackberries
* Cantaloupe
* Honeydew
* Lemons
* Limes
* Passionfruit
* Strawberries
* Watermelon

Other

* Eggs
* Vanilla extract (unsweetened)
* Spices like chili, nutmeg, cinnamon, ginger, cloves, and allspice
* Coconut (unsweetened, of course)
* Flax seed
* Herbs such as mint, lavender, and tarragon

Let's play with some options. While these aren't desserts you'll need your slow-cooker for, it's nice to know you can have something else stewing in it while you experiment with fresh and healthy dessert recipes!

Berry Medley

Fresh berries are loaded with flavor, especially when they're in season. Serve them with unsweetened whipped cream so the natural sweetness is allowed to really shine through.

Makes 2 servings.

½ cup fresh strawberries, sliced
½ cup blueberries
1 cup heavy cream

1. Put the sliced strawberries and blueberries in a bowl and stir to combine.

2. In a separate bowl, beat the heavy cream on high until it forms stiff peaks. Distribute the berries among 2 bowls and top with whipped cream.

Variations:

* Thicken the whipped cream by beating in 2 tablespoons of cream cheese, and flavor it with a splash of vanilla extract or unsweetened rum extract.
* Garnish with fresh mint.

Tropical Fruit Medley

This might not be the fruit salad you remember from childhood, but considering the low carb count it's a great substitute! Topping the sweet but soft fruits with crunchy coconut flakes and flax seeds provides flavor and texture.

1 small cantaloupe, ripe flesh cut into cubes

1 small honeydew melon, ripe flesh cut into cubes

1 passionfruit, sliced

1 cup unsweetened coconut flakes

½ cup flax seed

1. Combine the cantaloupe, honeydew, and passionfruit in a bowl. Stir to combine well.

2. Divide among 4 dishes. Sprinkle with the coconut flakes and flax seeds.

Variation:

* Spice this dish up a bit by adding ¼ teaspoon ground ginger to the coconut flakes and flax in a small bowl. Stir well to combine, and sprinkle the combo over the fruit.

Chocolate Cream Dream

Velvety and rich, a few spoonfuls of this delicious mixture will satisfy your craving for something sweet.

4 oz cream cheese

2 eggs

4 tablespoons unsweetened cocoa powder

1 teaspoon unsweetened rum extract

1. Beat the eggs. Soften the cream cheese by putting it in a small bowl and microwaving it for about 30 seconds. Add it to the beaten eggs and stir thoroughly to combine.

2. Microwave the cream cheese and egg mixture for 30 seconds, stir, and finish in the microwave for another 30 seconds. Stir to cool some, then stir in the cocoa powder and rum extract.

Variation:

✳ Make an orange-cinnamon cream by substituting unsweetened orange extract for the rum extract, and adding a teaspoon or so of cinnamon. The fruit-flavored cream is a great topping for blueberries.

Sweetened Coconut

Don't get too excited by the title of this dessert—it's not the sugar-saturated flakes you're used to finding on coconut cake. But it does make for a sweet change to the routine of unsweetened coconut, and it's chewy and delicious to add to many of the other dessert suggestions in this chapter.

Makes 1 to 6 servings.

1 cup unsweetened coconut
3 tablespoons water, boiling
1 teaspoon maple sugar

1. Put the coconut in a small bowl.

2. In a separate small dish, mix the maple sugar into the boiling water, stirring until dissolved. Pour the sugar water on the coconut and mix well.

3. Cover the bowl with plastic wrap to trap the steam and retain the moisture. Let the mix sit for at least 15 minutes. Stir. Allow to cool, and eat as either a treat on its own, or use it to top fresh fruit.

Maple sugar is dehydrated maple syrup. It contains only 2.7 grams/teaspoon. Used sparingly, it adds very few carbs, and retains the all-natural goodness of maple.

Chocolate Mousse à Vocado

Yes, indeed—this is chocolate mousse made with avocados! They are a creamy, dense, fruit that mashes into a lovely consistency. Make sure the avocados are ripe!

Makes 4 servings.

2 black-skinned (Haas) avocados

2 tablespoons butter, softened but not melted

½ cup unsweetened cocoa powder

1 teaspoon unsweetened vanilla extract

½ cup heavy cream

2 teaspoon maple sugar

1. Cut the avocados in half, remove the pits, and scoop the flesh into a bowl. Add the butter, cocoa powder, and vanilla extract and mash to combine well and until the consistency is smooth.

2. In a separate bowl, whip the heavy cream with the maple sugar until firm. Scoop out about ⅓ of it and fold it into the chocolate-avocado mix. Add another third, folding to thoroughly blend, then the remaining whipped cream.

3. Cover and refrigerate for about 30 minutes.

Dress up this dessert by dividing the mousse into wine glasses before refrigerating. Before serving, add a layer of sliced strawberries, top with a dollop of unsweetened whipped cream, and decorate with shavings of unsweetened chocolate.

Watermelon-Mint Towers

So refreshing, so colorful, and so summery! Enjoy!

Makes 2 servings.

1 thick slice watermelon, cut into cubes
2 sprigs fresh mint, leaves removed
Skewers

Build a watermelon "kabob" on the skewer by alternating a cube of fruit and a mint leaf until there are 4 or 5 cubes with mint leaves tucked between them. Face the skewer down toward the bottom of a plate to position the tower on the plate. Gently remove the skewer so the fruit tower is standing.

Variations:
* These towers are also delicious with cubes of honeydew melon alternated with the watermelon.
* For a creamy treat, dip the towers into unsweetened Greek yogurt.

Index

About Cider Mill Press
Book Publishers

Good ideas ripen with time. From seed to harvest, Cider Mill Press brings fine reading, information, and entertainment together between the covers of its creatively crafted books. Our Cider Mill bears fruit twice a year, publishing a new crop of titles each spring and fall.

Visit us on the Web at
www.cidermillpress.com
or write to us at
PO Box 454
12 Spring Street
Kennebunkport, Maine 04046